THE EDUCATION OF
SAM SANDERS

T. S. Poetter

Hamilton Books
A member of
The Rowman & Littlefield Publishing Group
Lanham · Boulder · New York · Toronto · Oxford

Copyright © 2006 by
T. S. Poetter

Hamilton Books
4501 Forbes Boulevard
Suite 200
Lanham, Maryland 20706
Hamilton Books Acquisitions Department (301) 459-3366

PO Box 317
Oxford
OX2 9RU, UK

Library of Congress Control Number: 2006922139
ISBN-13: 978-0-7618-3463-2 (paperback : alk. paper)
ISBN-10: 0-7618-3463-X (paperback : alk. paper)

This book is a work of fiction. Places, events, and situations
in this story are purely fictional. Any resemblance to actual
persons, living or dead, is coincidental.

ACKNOWLEDGEMENTS

I want to extend heartfelt thanks to several who made this project possible. Thank you to the community of scholars in the Curriculum and Pedagogy Group who supported this work with their early feedback on drafts shared at the group's annual conferences beginning in 2001. There is a very strong strand of scholarship in the group that supports the use of fiction among other arts as genres for communicating truths that we understand as scholar/activists to be vital in the fields of curriculum and educational reform. This group gave me wings to fly with the project…a chance to present, to hear feedback, and to use supportive criticism to improve the work. All of it improved the final product, this full-length novel that began as a fictional short and evolved into something much more over a five-year period. If you are interested in understanding more of my thinking about this project after reading the prologue and the book, please check out my book chapter entitled "Opening myself up to writing fiction" in Poetter, Haerr, Higgins, Hayes, & Wilson Baptist's (Eds.) *In(Ex)clusion: (Re)Visioning the Democratic Ideal* (2002 by Educator's International Press at http://www.edint.com/).

Several individuals played major roles throughout the process of getting this book from draft to press. Suffice it to say that they were confidants, critical readers, and tremendous supporters. I am indebted to them for their care and expertise, given freely: Catherine Haerr, Donna Breault, John Kornfeld, Jerry Allender, Kris Sloan, Tom Barone, Martha Whitaker, Kate Rousmaniere, Joe Norris, Deb Meier, Chris Higgins, Tom Romano, Steven Bauer, Ellen Bueschel, Richard Quantz, Susan Ohanian.

Thank you to all of my own students in undergraduate and graduate courses over the years that read drafts and gave feedback. Many provided inspiration and direction. Several deserve credit for urging me along. Kristi Hill, like many other undergraduates, loved Sam and told me so and kept me writing. Many of them expressed how unhappy they were with how Part One ended; they wanted more about Sam, and his future, and his school than I left them with in that early version. My forward momentum on this project was buoyed by student enthusiasm for the characters, the story, and the deeper messages I was attempting to convey about teaching and leadership and the future of public education. Catherine Haerr has continued to use some version of Sam in her teacher leadership courses at Miami University. She has invited me to many "Meet the Author" talks with her classes; these occasions always served as very important markers in the project for me. A spring 2004 curriculum course introduced me to Tom Crumbaker and Yvonne Douglas, students who inspired me to finish the book and gave me insights into the science that could bring the story home.

Amber Dingledine, an undergraduate in Middle Childhood Education and caregiver for our children, became a most trusted assistant on this project in the summer of 2004. She helped me put together book proposals and packets for review by publishers that ultimately landed me an agreement to publish this book with Hamilton Books. I thank her for her steadfastness and belief in the project.

Of course, Judith Rothman, Publisher and Friend, deserves all of the credit for seeing this project into print with Hamilton Books. When everyone else in the publishing world told me that this book was stuck between literary fiction and educational research and that it couldn't appear, Judy understood that this was exactly what I intended and that this book stood to make a contribution and would be read if it became available. My faith, supported by Judith, is in the readership; make what you will of this book, but understand that it is unlike other forms of literary fiction and educational scholarship. It attempts to bridge the art and science of educational research in order to get at some main ideas that are very worthy of scrutiny; it also gets at lives, and loves, and hopes, aspects of the human condition, which always go along with the science. We are human after all, especially in one of our most human of endeavors: Education.

Kim Logsdon of Avalanche Design, LLC in Oxford, Ohio, has been my formatter for several books. She painstakingly sees to it that I submit text that is clean, attractive, and readable.

Also, my wife Chris never read anything I wrote as a scholar until I had completed Part One of Sam. She's just never been interested in my professional writing. No matter how exciting I thought it was, she left it untouched. I never pushed it, but I wanted her to read Sam. I really wanted her feedback on this, to know if I was making a big mistake exploring fiction or if I had it in me to write, truly. I planted a copy of Part One where she couldn't avoid it and asked her please to read it and tell me what she thought of it. This went on for several months. Finally, to my surprise, she read Part One in one sitting, while sunning out back on a late spring day. She cried at the end of it, and I knew I had something that needed more attention. Her tears constituted one of the greatest gifts I've ever received. She identified with the characters and the story. They were alive, at last, in someone besides me.

Finally, I want my boys Mitch and Sam to know that no matter what happens with this book, whether anyone reads it or not, part of my professional life is wrapped up in the complex mess of trying to do something worthwhile with whatever gifts I have in the wider world. I hope to leave the world a little better for them, and for their children. I don't know how possible it is to trace any success in this area causally; all I know is that I'm trying my best – as a writer, as a teacher, as a leader, as a coach, as a father, son, and husband – and I hope they see that my effort, in part, is inspired by their very lives and the great potential they hold both to be productive members of society and to be loved by their parents, families, friends, and community.

To each reader, thanks for reading this book, and for helping to save public education in the 21st century. I acknowledge how critical you are to any movement toward something better.

Thomas S. Poetter
Oxford, Ohio
Spring 2006

PROLOGUE

I wrote *The Education of Sam Sanders* for several reasons.

I wanted to challenge anyone interested in where public schools are going to imagine what it would be like if the current crazes of standardizing the curriculum and testing children to death played themselves out to their "logical" conclusions. That is, what if we actually put children in a room with computer terminals and a facilitator for eight hours a day and made them consume a standardized, personality-less curriculum on-line so that they could improve merely at plugging and chugging answers to inane questions regarding standardized knowledge?

What if we built a rewards structure around the curriculum and the tests that became irresistible, and ultimately so "natural," that we couldn't imagine any alternatives? What if corporate American developed such a stranglehold on the day-to-day functioning of schooling that schooling lost its unique character as a great leveler, a teacher of democracy, the connective tissue between children, their communities, and the greater good that is the American project sans business, money, wealth, power, and greed? What if the picture of Downing School before Sam's revolution constituted the substance of nearly every student's schooling experience in America? What would it look like, feel like? What would it make us yearn for instead?

I could have written a research article about how the future is now, especially in Ohio where thousands of students are already stuck in these types of "virtual academies." I could have waxed on about how virtual pirates deliver sub-standard school experiences, basically stealing taxpayers' money out from under them through false promises of school improvement, and about how warehousing children is more convenient, less work, and for the entrepreneur more lucrative than working it out each day face-to-face like today's teachers, and administrators, and parents do in our public schools. But I didn't want to write a straight, non-fiction essay on the future of public education <u>that no one reads</u>. Instead, I wanted to stir things up, imagine wider possibilities, and draw the reader in. I felt fiction, as a genre, offered a way to do this. Whether anyone reads it or not is another story. Since you made it this far, you are one of the many I hope will do something with the book after reading it and enjoying it, like sharing it with others or acting on its major ideas yourself.

All of this begs the question of whether or not it's even right for an author like me, one who typically writes research articles and books, to use fiction as a tool for social and political ends so easily gleaned and interpreted from the book. I have struggled with this problem throughout the project. Great fiction writers claim that beginning with an agenda for the characters or even the story is a sure way to create something that is not genuine, even perhaps <u>flat</u> out of the box, at worst no better

The Education of Sam Sanders

than "uninteresting."

But this is where the story started for me: with a passionate will to call attention to the great tragedy of our era in education, that the winners today are creating schools and cultures in which the work of teaching and learning is distant from human lives: more technical, and less humane, organic; more tightly standardized, and less focused on exploration, discovery, and wander/wonder; more enamored with the ends of education as they yield goods and opportunities, and less on the means, processes, on how we get there and how we attend to ends all along the way, adjusting as we go; more about knowledge and facts, and less about lives, and, at root, relationships.

In the end, I had to go where my passion led me, and this meant that I'd follow Sam Sanders and Pete Willson through their first set of adventures together. No matter where they were heading and/or to what degree I had an end to their story in my head before I even started, the texture and possibilities of these characters and their story won the day. Yes, I have socio-political purposes in mind: the fall of the standardization and testing regimes as they impact public education as we know it in the United States of America at the post-dawning of the 21st century. I also have in mind a progressive reclamation of the classroom and our thinking about education and schooling, one that puts students and their lives at the center of our endeavors. And yes, I think you can see the possibilities more clearly, more dynamically, through the life and times of Sam and Pete than you can through ours in the present. I hope you find at the end of your reading here that these ideas resonate for you and that the characters and the story stirred you to different levels of understanding and thinking on the issues at hand.

Quite frankly, I also said to myself, "You can write, so take a shot at writing this story." While I understand and respect the role and the task of the fiction writer, I felt like I could tackle it and that on future attempts I'd get even better at it. But you have to start somewhere, and first efforts can be good, solid. This is the positive feeling I kept inside me all the way through the writing and the publishing of this book. It was a tremendous experience, and I'm glad I took this pathway.

I wanted to highlight several things I believe to be true about human beings living and working together in communities like schools and small towns. I believe that individuals have a tremendous amount of power, especially as their lives grow to carry moral and ethical weight, like the lives of Sam Sanders, Pete Willson, Dr. Dormont, and Ms. Belders, for instance, do. I believe that children get it much more deeply and richly than we give them credit for; they know when they are being duped, cheated, and they know when they are in the presence of the "real deal." Perhaps the cynical side of us sees the lives of children tipping toward the age-old adult images of them: that they are lazy, will do anything to play and not work, and will always choose the least strenuous road toward any destination. Anyone who has worked with children lately sees these things sometimes, but when they see them they rarely ask how the experiences and demands foisted on children, in schools for instance, perhaps themselves contribute mightily to the results we don't like. Anyone would also see children who are driven, motivated, curious, and bright as well. I would contend that all youths' make-ups lie in these categories; it's just that we are typically blind to the truth about their lives, and we don't see the possibilities, the potential. But they see things much more clearly than we do, and sometimes, like Sam, they will take the risk of making their truth the true reality at hand.

I contend that teachers have a great deal of power to make change. Currently, teachers aren't organized to create the conditions for change in the curriculum and in teaching. They are organized as labor groups, with barriers built up over decades between them and communities and administrators and students in order to protect valuable labor and economic rights. But at some point, they must organize themselves to battle the standardization and testing regimes or they will become obsolete in spite of themselves, like Pete Willson did before he realized after 20 years that he had become a walking, talking mechanical tool of the state whose primary function is to turn on/off machines and monitor their use.

It's possible to change your personal and professional course in mid-stream or even at the end without throwing it all away. Pete and Dormont do risk losing their careers in teaching and administering. They live and work in an environment where someone like Mr. Stevens has a lot of power to create havoc, to oust people, no less. But they realize again that they are the professionals, that the systems they put in place have a human face (especially in this case in the courts), and that once history and possibility and events seem set in stone, a sword can still be pulled from a place where it had been impossibly set still and fast. They are willing to take risks with their lives – not silly, uncalculated ones, but risks born out of true commitment and vision. We all need to take more public risks to defend what's right. For instance, it's not right to warehouse children and adults in institutions where narrow, privileged knowledge is the only commodity of worth. I'd like to see us rectify that; my voice, in this form, is pushing us toward change. There are many ways to take action for change; perhaps you will lift your voices and take action for better in your own setting.

I also wanted to put the spotlight on teaching. Something rather magical and somewhat mysterious happens when good teaching takes place. Students get energized, projects soar, and new knowledge gets born. Sometimes children who inquire, like Rex Houndson, discover that peril lurks and that their findings can save the day, even human lives. One of the things that haunts me, personally, is the prospect of the current generation of teachers and the ones coming after them not having any idea about how to create and deliver curriculum in any but a standardized, rote fashion. I'm awake at nights wondering what might happen to us when the last progressive educator dies and no one left in teaching or in education has a clue about how to set up a problem for children to solve or about creating opportunities simply for students to experience the world together in unique ways and then to discuss the ramifications of those experiences for becoming more completely human and a better citizen. Maybe no one will remain who can get to Rex Houndson.

I've been asked on numerous occasions: Who is the target audience for this book? I'm hesitant to answer because I think the book has to do with all of us and that everyone should read it, to the tune of the millions J.K. Rowling turns on with her Harry Potter books! While I know that Potter is a different beast, of course, and that my delusions of grandeur won't sell any books, I do intend for a wide readership. The book has the potential for crossover appeal between young adults and adults. I think teachers and students of teaching can gain a lot from reading the book and discussing it together. Teacher educators in pre-service and in-service programs should use the book; it can be used to get the ball rolling on practical issues surrounding teaching and learning and on broader policy-related issues. I think parents and community groups should use the book as a discussion starter about the future of public education.

If the book is used in a course with novice and/or veteran teachers or both, the book should be used as a literary piece with the goal of creating a dialogic window for discussing issues surrounding policy and practice in curriculum and teaching. The teacher should employ questioning techniques about the motives of the characters, the steps they take toward change, the impact of the actions they take, a comparison of conditions in classrooms and in teaching today as compared with this more futuristic vision, etc.

Ultimately, like most language arts teachers know about a good book, it can often teach itself. This much is true with my early experiences of using Sam Sanders with teachers: They will read and enjoy the book. If you have any reasonably similar experiences to the ones I've had with the book, it will spur deep debate, opposition, calls to action, and new ways of thinking. Isn't this what we want out of any type of text we use in an educative setting? Perhaps it's what some of us want out of a book we simply read for pleasure as well.

At any rate, I have plans for Sam. I intend to follow his life through high school and college. I see two more books on the horizon before I let go. Right now, Sam has his teeth into my ankle and won't let go; perhaps his bite will be worse than his bark in the long-run, in terms of the societal and political uproar over where public education is heading today. In the end, public education is worth saving. We need the dynamic lives of institutions and people shaping citizens' lives. But what form will that interaction take? What will we study together? How will we teach and learn? We are destroying public education by making it so tightly wound around standards and tests. There are other, better ways to organize schooling for teaching and learning. Teachers and administrators know how to do it; it's high time we support them in righting the ship. They, along with parents and students, are the only ones who can.

PREFACE – A NOTE FROM MISSY TALLONS

I'm Missy Tallons, a veteran reporter for the *Record-Star* newspaper, which serves two counties and several small towns, including Downing where the following story takes place. I don't live in Downing, I actually live in Fletcher, about six miles down the road. But I've spent lots of time in Downing and know the folks over there pretty well. You'll get to know me a little bit as a result of reading this account about a boy named Sam Sanders and his school, Downing School. I tried to make the story as little as possible about me, though some of what I think and experienced creeps in at points.

I have covered education stories for the paper for most of my more than 20 years on the job. I've seen a lot in public education and I thought that I had seen everything I was going to see with regard to public schools until I witnessed first-hand what happened in Downing last spring. These things surprised me, and so did my reaction to them. When I first published accounts of what happened at Downing in *The Record-Star,* I tried to remain objective, tried to report just the facts. But as I dug deeper, I realized another story needed to be told, one that lay below the surface of what people did and said during that time.

As a result, I break some of my own writing rules here. I don't just give a factual account of what supposedly happened. Instead, based on extensive interviews with townspeople and my own time spent in the setting, I re-create the story so that it reads more like a novel than like a newspaper account. I realize that I might get beat up by critics from the papers who say I have no business venturing into this sort of thing, writing a story that's more than a newspaper story. I realize that writers of other non-fiction narratives and fiction itself will no doubt take exception to my writing as well, a newspaper hack perhaps trying to do more than I should with what seems like a small story on the surface. But, as most writers will tell you, when the story has to get out, the author has little choice than to get out of the way and tell it.

So here goes.

PART ONE:

THE EDUCATION OF SAM SANDERS

1 – GETTING THERE IS THE HARDEST PART

A child's ball rolled suspiciously free across the lonely rural road, right in front of Pete Willson's rattletrap pickup. He was driving too fast, but slowed down just in time to stop on the lazy stretch of road and watch the ball roll silently from left to right, first over the lip of the highway on the left and then as the ball nestled itself on the other side of the road against some tall, unmown spring grass. "Gee wiz, Willson, slow down. You're going to kill someone someday," he scolded himself.

Pete, or Mr. Willson to the 28 waiting eighth graders down the road at Downing School, noticed the ball's markings, typical of a $6.99 grocery store-bought plastic ball, the kind you get out of those big bins in the aisle next to the $10 frozen dinners. The ball had those scratchy marks all around it from excessive use, more than a ball like that could usually take before finding a nail or a dog's eager mouth to end its life. This one had red, white, and blue markings on it, a white band around its middle with fading blue stars imbedded in the band. Before it stopped in the grass, the ball had a sort of bound to it, rolling slowly at first and then picking up steam, and then jumping playfully as it hit a pebble or two on its way to the other side.

He looked alertly back to the left, leaving the ball for now in its final resting place; it had completed its journey. He sat there in the middle of the road quizzing the landscape as he placed his coffee back in the cup holder, turned down the radio, rolled down his window, and listened. He did all of these things simultaneously, practically, his hands working well together in that urgent set of moments. If he knew anything at all, he knew there would be somebody chasing after the ball. No wind had blown the ball down the driveway on his left. No dog played there, lurching at the ball from the grassy yard. "There must be a child attached to it," Pete thought, "and it must be Sam Sanders."

Pete looked particularly hard for Sam Sanders, the boy who lived in the house at the end of the driveway. He knew the house, because he knew Sam. Sam sat in the fourth row, third seat back in Pete's eighth grade class at Downing School, set to open with the first bell in only 20 short minutes. He still had about a mile or two to go to the school, with time running out.

Mr. Willson sometimes ran late, but he always made it to school on time to meet his students before the first bell. He hadn't missed a day of school or showed up late for years. He made a calculated judgment while looking at his watch: "Just a few moments left to get Sam to school on time today. A very important day." He turned into the drive and made his way up to the house.

He parked his truck near the open garage and stepped out, one leg remaining uncommitted on the running board of the cab, calling out for Sam in his best teacher voice, "Hey, Sam? Lose your ball? Come on, time for school." But no one answered, nothing around the place even moved until Sam's mom, Betsy Sanders, appeared at the door of the screened-in front porch a few moments later. She surprised Pete, actually, standing there suddenly, holding a skillet, drying it slowly with a towel.

"Well, Mr. Willson. Why don't you come on in? Sam's not here, but we've got some eggs here and some bacon left. I'll heat 'em right up."

"No, thank you, Ms. Sanders, I just saw Sam's ball roll across the road and I thought he'd surely be following it. Do you know where he is? We've got to get to school. Big day, you know, with the students taking the practice test."

"No, I sure don't know where he is. I sent him out around 7:30. Said he wasn't feeling so good, so he went back to the barn to read. Can't seem to get him to put them books down. He likes it back there in the barn. It's quiet, you know, and warm after a good breakfast. You sure you're not comin' in, Mr. Willson?"

"I'm sure, thanks Ma'am. I'll just check around back for Sam, if you don't mind. We'll be late today if we're not careful."

"No, I don't mind, Mr. Willson. You check all around, and you stop back anytime."

"Thanks, Ms. Sanders," he called back, "Yes, I sure will come back," he added, not as an afterthought, but for effect, sensing that he had impressed her somehow and knowing Mr. Sanders had passed, gone now two years, the victim of a deadly combination: heavy drinking, a dark, rainy night, a fast car, and a light pole. Mr. Sanders had been Mr. Willson's student, too, some years before.

He stepped out of the truck, less guarded now, but knowing he couldn't wander far with school starting any minute.

Back in the Sanders' barn, not far from the house, there was no trace of the boy except for a worn out copy of Twain's *Huck Finn* sitting on top of one of the animal stalls. "That's funny," Pete thought out loud, "Twain's not on Sam's grade-level reading list. I wonder what he's reading that for after all we've been through?"

He carried the book back to the truck and made his way to school, pulling into the parking lot just a little too fast. The crossing guard, a sixth grader, gave him the evil eye and scribbled something on her report pad. "Another parking lot violation, and one step closer to hurting someone," he thought, smiling at the guard, hoping she'd stop writing but knowing she wouldn't. He walked like an Olympic speed walker up the front path to the school.

He raced past the principal, Dr. Dormont, eking out a "good morning" to her.

"Mr. Willson, nice to see you. Big day," she commanded.

Mr. Willson – now racing with the tightest and fastest of walks down the long hallway to 4B, where his class, he hoped, waited for him – heard the first bell sounding.

2 – TEST DAY

"Good morning class," Mr. Willson said, short of breath and red-faced as he entered the classroom, talking over the din of bells sounding and students milling about.

"Good morning, Mr. Willson," the class echoed back, while settling into their seats for the day.

Mr. Willson scanned the class and the desks for Sam Sanders. No Sam Sanders.

"Anyone seen Sam?" Mr. Willson asked the class.

A chorus of "no's" ricocheted off the walls of the room as the students made their ways to desks and coat racks. Pete glanced around, taking attendance as he counted heads and named the familiar names.

As he worked to gather his papers and to get ready to administer the test, a moving object caught his eye out the window. It was a boy on a bike, Sam Sanders no less, zooming his way past on his old stingray, standing with his rear end off the seat, legs pumping hard, headed down the road, past the school driveway, and out of sight.

Mr. Willson watched Sam ride out of sight. He didn't move until Sandra Boyle tapped his shoulder, "Mr. Willson, are you all right, sir? All of us are ready for the test, and the loudspeaker said we all should get in our seats and get ready…Mr. Willson? I'm sorry I'm out of my seat, sir," she tapped his shoulder harder, "Mr. Willson?"

He snapped to, but his hopes for the test sank with the sight of Sam peddling away. He couldn't chase after Sam, and he couldn't leave the children with the test starting. He had to give the test.

"Okay, class, your computer screens should be prompting you to begin the reading test…now. Begin and I'll speak with you in three hours. We'll do the math test after lunch. Remember, this is important. Do your best – the best *I know* that you all can do."

Mr. Willson placed his hand against the scoring machine next to his desk to begin the test. The machine read the chip implanted in his palm, and automatically began giving the test to the students on their individual screens at their desks. The test activation process always gave him a warm feeling. It reminded him of the importance of his work as a teacher, how much it counted. It made him feel safe, as if things occurred with some order, and on time. All that the students had been learning in his class would come out now; the test would show what the students knew.

He stared down at his terminal showing how the students were doing on the questions as they progressed through the test. He saw them doing well, and miserably, as their right and wrong answers tabulated in a continuous fashion right before his eyes. The scores go directly to the state computer; the state closely monitored each test site by computer and by camera. He could not coach the students in any way, shape, or form; he couldn't give them any sorts of cues or prompts. As he watched the test taking shape he thought, "Oh, Steven, that's a careless mistake. The commas go inside the quotation marks in that sentence." All the while he knew that the computer couldn't tabulate a score for Sam, and that Sam's "0" would count against the class, and against him.

Drifting off now, a bit dazed by the screen and the length of the test, Pete let his eyes go to the tattered cover of *Huck Finn,* which had made it all the way from Sam Sanders' barn stall to Pete's classroom desk. He hadn't seen a copy of the book in years. The school put books on the computer now, usually just representative parts of them, hardly ever the whole thing, cover to cover. He opened the book and turned the pages to one of his favorite passages, one that stuck with him all these years. He didn't have any trouble finding it:

> "It's so (Pap Finn said to Huck). You can do it (read). I had my doubts when you told me. Now looky here; you stop that putting on frills. I won't have it. I'll lay for you, my smarty; and if I catch you about that school I'll tan you good. First thing you know you'll get religion, too. I never see such a son."

Then he felt guilty for the pleasure the book brought, especially about how it felt in his hands, rubbing rough against his fingertips and lying gently in his palm. He felt bad about the ideas the book stirred up again, and he put the book down and turned back to the screen.

Where in the world was Sam Sanders?

3 – PEDALING HOME

Sam pedaled as fast as he could. He had taken the long way around to the main road that went into town, right past the school and into harm's way. He knew the risks in pedaling past the school. The sheriff's deputy might see him and scoop him up, and deliver him to the truant officer, or worse yet, right to Mr. Willson. But he saw the sheriff deputy's car sitting empty in front of the school. He saw no other movement as he pedaled, outside or inside the school for that matter. He felt odd, though, as if he had been seen. A heat pricked the back of his neck as he turned his gaze back to the open road. He thought, "Keep pedaling, keep pedaling."

"Maybe I sort of want to get caught," he thought briefly as he coasted for a moment, "like criminals sometimes do, returning to the scene of the crime."

People thought of Sam Sanders as an exceptional boy in so many ways. He often reflected like this on his life, on the things that happened or didn't happen to him, or on the things that might have come about, even as a boy of only 13 years. Adults liked him because he carried on unusually intelligent conversations with them. Kids liked him because of his sense of humor and because he liked to do things such as ride his bike and play ball. While he had a penchant for reading nearly everything he could get his hands on, including books he checked out of the public library – a practice so rare that many people found it a bit odd and even talked suspiciously about it behind his and his mother's backs – he enjoyed a wide acceptance by people in the small town of Downing.

A cold sweat dripped down onto the tip of his nose as he rode into town. Making a furious dash with a stingray bike didn't really fulfill Sam's sense of the theatrical and really tired him out. The truth is, he had no other transportation, no other choice. The bottom line really is a bottom line sometimes: he just couldn't bear the thought of sitting for six hours of a day like this one, or of any day for that matter, in front of a computer screen taking a test on reading. He filled his life with Twain and King and Rowling, on his own, which made what happened in school pale in comparison. He couldn't imagine another unbearable round of hours spent reading about the cutting of timberlands up north or answering questions about the size of the lumberjack's saw or the distance from the log camp to the river, A, B, C, D, or E.

"Speaking of which," he thought as he slowed down a bit now, turning onto the town's main road and onto the sidewalk that bordered the big houses on Main Street, "where's *Huck Finn*?" He toyed with the books in his front carrier, moving them around to reveal their titles as he miraculously balanced the bike and kept pedaling. He soon realized, "No *Huck Finn.*"

"Darn it, I must have left him in the barn. Oh well, I'll just have to make this trip again tomorrow then."

He decided he should stop talking to himself, what with the town center getting closer. More people stirred on the town's streets than near the school on the outskirts. They walked their dogs and picked up their morning papers in their driveways. He saw Mr. Stevens, his dad's former boss at the plant and a school board member, walking down his front walk in his robe and slippers to get the paper, one of life's remaining simple pleasures, almost as good as riding a stingray bike. Sam recognized him from past holiday parties at the plant, and the time Mr. Stevens came to his house to discuss something or other with his dad a few years back. He tried to act like he didn't see Stevens, his focus on pedaling intensifying, he furrowed his brow and focused on the road, but Mr. Stevens called out in his direction, all cordial-like, as he bent down and up in one motion, now with his paper in hand, "Sam Sanders? How you doin' son?"

Sam had to look and respond or the game would end. Maybe it was over already. "Oh, hey Mr. Stevens. I'm fine. How you doin'?" and he put his head down to avoid an answer and kept pedaling.

"Good, son. Shouldn't you be pedaling the other way, to school?" his voice trailing off as Sam sped away.

Sam heard Mr. Stevens' final question, of course, but he kept riding, not looking back. Pedaling.

When he got to his destination in the middle of town, he practically rammed his bike into the concrete steps leading up to the small red brick building. He scooped up the books from his carrier and scampered up the steps. The sign on the front door read, "Open," and he whispered a soft, victorious, "Yes!" under his breath as he entered the town library.

4 – FOUR MORE BOOKS

Ms. Belders, the librarian, sitting in her usual place at the front desk, looked down at a book through her reading glasses, the kind of glasses that perch on the end of your nose and that you look over when you want to talk to somebody or to give them a dirty look for being loud. She shifted her whole weight in her chair with a sigh of relief that Sam seemed okay, as well as a sigh of trepidation, knowing that Sam's presence there meant truancy. Sam wasn't a chronic truant, but a surgical truant, missing school occasionally, specifically to pursue other more important matters to him, like reading. On days like this, he often landed at the library, right in front of Ms. Belders.

"So, Mr. Sanders, here we are again. What's the occasion this time?"

"Test day," Sam said as he dropped the books into the return bin and purposefully made his way to the fiction aisles.

"Oh, no. Test day. I should have known," Ms. Belders said, pursing her lips and putting down her book. She began the two-step routine of giving Sam a polite scolding and calling the school. She got up, slowly, and reached for the phone.

"Ms. Belders, just let me have these four more books? Please, before I have to go, maybe just this one last time?"

"When is there going to be a last time for you, Sam? You're like a junkie, you know," she quipped as she dialed the phone. She mumbled something or other on the phone to Mr. Jones, the truant officer at the school, and Sam walked casually up to her counter.

"Listen, Sam," Ms. Belders said softly, looking him right in the eye, "you know how much I like you coming in here. It would be a pretty lonely place without you," her voice echoing against the books and the walls and the floors. "But you can't continue to miss school, especially on test days. You know how important it is to take the tests; they mean so much to the school and to your future."

"I just want these four books, please, Ms. Belders," Sam said, handing them up to her at the counter. As usual, he ignored her basic message, he had heard it all before. But this time he noticed something different in her tone of voice and in her gaze. Worry. "Something's wrong, Ms. Belders. What is it?" he asked.

"People are talking, and the other children are growing more restless in school, Sam. Why can't you just do your assignments *in* school and read *after* school?"

At that moment, they both saw Mr. Jones, the truant officer, walking halfway up the steps with Mr. Stevens, still in his robe and slippers and holding his newspaper, pointing up to the library door with it before turning around and heading for home. Mr. Stevens, the great informant, citizen of the century.

"Mr. Stevens. I knew it," Sam said, under his breath, but loud enough for Ms. Belders to hear.

Ms. Belders smiled, and noticed Sam placing the library's new pocket version of Shakespeare's *Romeo and Juliet* in his back pocket. It wasn't one of the allotted four books he had chosen to check out. Criminal as the act was, she said nothing. Then she handed him his four new books and said, "Two weeks, then you can get *four* more."

Mr. Jones walked in and took off his hat, tipping it to Ms. Belders, "Good morning, Ma'am."

"Mr. Jones? What a surprise." Mr. Jones, with his shoulders ever slumping, rather begrudgingly readied himself to read Sam the riot act and take him into custody.

5 – A COLD, HARD REALITY

Sam had never ridden in a police car before. He had always imagined riding in the back of one someday, along for a ride with two cops chasing some criminals, talking to the cops, maybe holding a tape recorder or camera and taking it all in so he could write a story about his experiences for a newspaper or a magazine.

"What's the deal, Mr. Jones? Why the Sheriff's car today? Where's your car?"

"Deputy's just lazing around the school and said I could take the cruiser, and besides, you're a top priority pickup, what with the test going on at school today. I'm 'deputized' myself, too, you know."

"I'm not taking the test today, Mr. Jones. I'd rather read."

"Well, son, that's not possible, really. Everyone has to take the test sooner or later. The school is depending on it. Don't you know what can come into a school with high test scores, about the bonuses hard-working teachers can make, about the real estate values that improve with your best performance? You can never make that up to us if you don't take the test and contribute a high score, which everyone knows you would be able to do."

"What's the last book you read, Mr. Jones?" Sam asked. Mr. Jones took the question in stride.

"Son, books are for people who live *out* of reality. I live *in* reality, every day. The real world – the good and bad of it – all of it, I see it in this job. I don't have time for books. How can books help me in this work anyway? I read all the time, manuals and such. They help me do a better job protecting the public from truants, and truants from themselves. That's what I get paid for, that's what I live for. You could have a good job like I do, too, if you followed the rules and did your school work. You'd go far, I think, Sam Sanders."

"No, Mr. Jones, the last book?" Sam persisted.

"Well, I guess it's been awhile, really, I guess I can't remember."

"Well," Sam said calmly, "I think you used to read a lot, but don't anymore." Sam said this while turning away from Mr. Jones and looking out the window at the quiet streets of the town, past Mr. Stevens' house and out toward the school. Sam had been looking at Mr. Jones' face in the rearview mirror as he drove, like a passenger who might steal glances at the chauffeur as they conversed on a short trip to the airport.

"I think Mr. Willson, my teacher, used to read a lot, too. I read in one book where teachers used to actually use books in school. Kids would read them, and then write about them, maybe even write a poem or draw a picture or put on a play

about the book. Wouldn't that be something, Mr. Jones? When's the last time you
went to a play?"

"A play? Well, now, I suppose it's been even longer than it's been since I read
a book, Sam. Why are you asking me all this? Don't you know you're the one who
should be interrogated?"

"Yeah, well, I'm thinking maybe you'd like to read this book," and he handed
the book from his back pocket over the seat to Mr. Jones, who fumbled around with
it before being able to read the title.

"*Romeo...and...Juliet.* I think I've heard of that. Shakespeare, or something,
right? Made into a movie or something, wasn't it, way back?"

"Right, Mr. Jones. Shakespeare. You'll like it. Tell me what you think about it
next week. I'm sure I'll be seeing you around some."

"Okay, kid, okay," Mr. Jones said as he put the book down on the front seat
and pulled into the school parking lot. "Now let's go see Dr. Dormont. She's eager
to have a little talk with you herself. And not about books."

6 – THE TEST AWAITS

Mr. Jones confiscated Sam's books immediately; books weren't used in school anymore. Books made too much clutter and students always forgot them or just left them in their lockers or at home on purpose. But that happened way back when teachers and students used books in class. Now students could find everything they needed for school on the computer. The state gave each child in each school access to the state database, with all the necessary reading materials and drill worksheets and homework assignments. The database has everything a student needs to do well in school and on the tests. The schools made every effort to streamline students' work so they wouldn't be distracted from the information they needed to learn in order to score well on the tests. Sam Sanders, and his books, had become a distraction.

Sam had handed his books over to Mr. Jones, knowing full well that Jones had become an ally and that Sam would get the books back, that they wouldn't be returned directly to Ms. Belders at the library. He smiled, and walked into the school office with Mr. Jones to see Dr. Dormont.

"Sam Sanders. I'm glad you're safe and sound. Welcome back," she said, with just a touch of sarcasm.

She turned her attention to Mr. Jones, "And thank you, Mr. Jones. That will be all," she said, dismissing him from the room. He shut the door behind him. Sam sat down in one of the two chairs facing the desk.

Dr. Dormont sat down behind her desk, and folded her hands in front of her, took a deep breath, and started her speech, "Sam, let me get right to the point. We need you to take the eighth grade test today. If we average scores of 86 for the reading and 77 for the math, we get an extra $10 million for building improvements and teacher salaries from the state. That's just for the practice test. The big bonuses come with the end of year test in early June. We need your scores, Sam. I made an arrangement with the state to allow you to take the test in the media center, alone and undistracted. Let's go."

She rose and stepped toward the door, her signal for Sam to get up and go with her.

Instead, Sam replied, still seated, "Dr. Dormont, I'm not taking the test today. I hate those tests. I hate the boring stories, the questions, I hate how long it takes to read everything for one little detail that you have to choose out of a lineup of answers. I'd really rather be reading on my own, or writing something for that matter."

"Son," she continued to come out from behind her desk now, after pausing for his answer, and sat in the seat next to him in the companion chair, "I knew your father, and I know your mother, very well. They both went to school here and they did well. Your father was a very special student, bright and kind and all. But the books he read, they changed him. You know he read a lot, too, don't you, Sam? Books got him in trouble at work and then, well, you know, all the rest."

"Yes, Ma'am, I know all the rest," Sam replied, unhesitating. "He and I used to read together, and talk, long into the night sometimes, about the things in the books, and about us. He was a little sad sometimes, but I loved him."

"I guess I'm not saying that you shouldn't have loved him, but the books, Sam, they were a flaw. They got in the way," said Dr. Dormont, desperate now, beginning to plead. "They were like a drug, Sam, and he couldn't stop. And we did everything here that we knew how to help him. Won't you let us help you, let us try to make up for us going wrong with your dad?"

"I'm not taking the test, Dr. Dormont. I'm sorry to be disrespectful, but I read once in a history book that students and parents once had the right to *not* take the tests, or to *not* have their scores counted, either way, whether they took the test or not. Don't you think students and schools should have some options, Dr. Dormont? If we don't have any options, then what are we doing?"

Icy, and straightforward, she said with a finality in her tone that he had never heard from her before, "Sam, you are going to take that test. *You* don't have any options. *We* don't have any options. The only option we have is to lose, and we're not going to do that. I don't know where you got all of these crazy ideas, but they are damaging. Now, let's go."

"No, ma'am, I'm not going."

"Then I'll have to call your mother, as a last resort. She doesn't need this from you, dredging up all those memories and the pain. It's time for you to be a man about this and do your duty."

"No." After a long pause, Dr. Dormont threw up her hands, walked out the door, and beckoned Mr. Jones to come in. He had been waiting right outside the door.

"Take him down to position 1, Mr. Jones. I'm going to call his mother."

7 – ONE VERY LONG DAY

No one likes waiting for the ax to fall or waiting for the flickering chance of being saved. But Sam waited at cubicle 1 (position 1, as Dr. Dormont liked to call it) in the media center, sitting in front of the computer, just staring at the screen. Mr. Jones had advised him that he could use any of the programs on the computer to review for the test, but he didn't have it in him. He couldn't bear the thought of it, sitting there all day taking that test or preparing for it. He nearly cried sitting there, alone, his spirit almost broken. But he knew his mother would be there soon. She, he hoped, would pick him up and whisk him away to safety.

She showed up about 20 minutes later, still wearing her morning dress, with a few stains left from the last few breakfasts, and a yellow scarf wrapped loosely around her neck. She had been escorted in by Mr. Jones, and then left alone with Sam at the cubicle. Sam saw Dr. Dormont peering hopefully through the glass door to the media center. Ms. Sanders pulled up a chair from cubicle 2 and said, "You've caused quite a stir this morning, Son, you know?"

"They want me to take the test, Mom. I said I wouldn't. They caught me with Ms. Belders down at the library. I never made a fuss, Mom, or nothin'. It's just I can't see wasting all my time here doing all this 'work' when it doesn't have anything to do with me. I probably don't know all of that stuff on the computer or on the test, and I don't really care to know it. What difference does it make anyway?"

After a rather long pause, Ms. Sanders replied, "You know, Sam, we've been going on like this for some time now. I'm not so sure I've been totally fair to you. I need to tell you several things that school can do for you. One of them is to teach you to live up to your responsibilities. Now, right or wrong, everyone has to take this test, and you're going to take it, just like I did, and just like your father did."

"Dad never took the test."

"What do you mean, he never took the test? He scored one of the highest scores ever on his eighth grade test. We were always very proud of that. Just ask Mr. Willson about it," she said, her voice rising. Sometimes Sam flustered her, making her already unraveled world unravel further.

"I did ask him about it, Mom. Mr. Willson said he took the test *for* Dad, because his conscience got the best of him. He couldn't let Dad fail, and not go to college. He says Dad never took tests well, that he was always daydreaming and giving answers off the charts on the tests, never to the point at all. I'm sorry, Mom, but I know the truth. Dad really was smart, and he read books, too. But he and Mr. Willson thought it was crazy for him not to be able to get a high score on the tests, so Mr. Willson just took the test for him. No harm done."

"No...harm...done...? Those are words that don't fit here, Son. All the harm in the world has been done. I just don't know what to do about it."

"I'm sorry, Mom, I didn't mean to upset you. What about the truth? Doesn't that mean something after all this time?"

"I need some time to figure that out, Sam. For now, it's back to school work for you. I'll see you at home tonight. I have a stop to make before going home."

And out the door she went, escorted by Mr. Jones and Dr. Dormont. Sam just sat there, relegated to hours of looking at the screen, until the final bell rang, and exhausted, lonely, bored to tears, he made his way on foot uptown to get his bike, and to make the long pedal home.

8 – POKING AROUND

It was a long ride home for Sam on his bike; it had taken him great distances that day. But he knew he had to go straight home, no detours. He had his books, at least, which Mr. Jones had given back to him on his way out the door of the school. Mr. Jones had been waiting for him, and even tapped the breast pocket of his jacket to indicate to Sam, with a nod attached for good measure, like Pip's Wemmick glorying in his "portable property," that he had the mini-Shakespeare in his safe possession as well.

Once home, Sam pedaled up the driveway and parked his bike a little more carefully than he had at the library that morning. He called out, "Hey, Mom, I'm home," like usual when he walked in the side door, but he didn't pursue a reply, or any type of face-to-face meeting with her. He thought he would steer clear of her, maybe just stay out of the way for awhile. She let him off the hook as well with her call back, "Oh, Hi Son, I'm in the basement tending to the laundry." She never did laundry in the late afternoon, always late at night.

After dropping his new books on his desk in his room, Sam went out to find his ball. He thought maybe he'd kick it a bit, throw it off the roof and catch it, maybe play a little trash can golf around the place to burn off some of the energy left unspent from his boring day at cubicle 1. But he couldn't find the ball across the road where he thought it would still be sitting. Balls that scooted down the driveway unretrieved usually set up a temporary home for the day on the other side of the road.

This ball had been irretrievable that morning, since it had clearly been on a collision path with Mr. Willson's truck. Sam saw that collision coming, after his great punt of the ball had bounded off the roof and then back over his head without him having a good chance to even slow it down, let alone catch it. He instinctively scanned left to right before he launched himself down the driveway after the ball, recognized Mr. Willson's rattletrap speeding toward him, and high-tailed it back to the barn, unseen he hoped, for his bike and toward his daylong journey. He never would have made it to the library if he had spoken to Mr. Willson about the ball. He would have wound up taking the test, no doubt, or compromising Mr. Willson again, a second generation to do so.

He continued the search for his ball in the front yard, where the grass was high and some old, rotting furniture had found its final home. Around back? No sign. But in the barn he found it, lying on the ground where he had dropped *Huck Finn.*

The morning's events came back to him now. He remembered not finding the book in his bike rack. He looked around the stalls and all over the barn for the book. Strange. No sign of it.

"It's bound to turn up," he thought. "Mom must have it."

Late afternoons drift away for boys Sam's age. Typically, a little ball playing and a little poking around in the barn filled his free time, and then he finished his chores: fed the few goats and milked their two cows, swept out the stalls, and cleaned up trash around the yard. By the time dinner hour came, about 5:30 at his house, he felt sufficiently worn out and tired and ready to settle in for one of his Mom's excellent meals, maybe chicken this time. As he made his way around the house one last time before the end of the day, he saw and heard Mr. Willson's pickup turning up the driveway.

9 – MR. WILLSON COMES TO DINNER

Sam hadn't seen Mr. Willson all day, since he spied his truck from a few hundred yards down that same road at 7:45 a.m. He wondered what Willson wanted.

Mr. Willson turned into the driveway too fast, but stopped short of running into anything, including Sam himself. He poked his head and his left arm out the window, holding a book up and asking, "You missing a book?" He stepped out of the truck and walked toward Sam.

"I found it in the barn this morning, Sam. Did your Mom tell you I came around looking for you? It was test day, you know. It's your book, right?"

"Yes, sir, I know. No, she didn't tell me you were coming. I haven't really talked to Mom yet tonight."

"She asked me over for dinner. That may be a little awkward, I know, but she's worried about you, Sam. She thought maybe I could help."

"Yeah, well maybe you can help. You ever read *Huck Finn*?"

"Many years ago, yes, Sam. Probably not a day goes by that I don't miss teaching books like that in class. We used to do that, you know, years ago."

"I know. Listen, maybe you can help me with the part about Pap Finn early in the book. I know it's Pap they find on the boat. He's dead, I know, I made it that far and get most of it. But I don't get why Pap doesn't want Huck to learn to read or to go to school? Why doesn't he want better for his son than he had?"

"Well, that's a little hard to explain, Sam," Mr. Willson said, crouching down like he was talking to a little kid, even though he knew he wasn't talking to a little kid anymore.

"You see…many years ago, going to school wasn't so common as it is now. Folks without the opportunity and life circumstances often didn't even learn to read. People who couldn't read had fewer opportunities in life, a lot like they do now if they don't master reading. Society treated low-lifes like Pap roughly. He had a tough life, having lost his wife and all and having a little son to raise. Heavy-drinking, illiterate lost souls who couldn't hold a job or tend to a family didn't offer society much. And they sometimes couldn't get past the pain of having their own offspring surpass their meager accomplishments. It's not like now, Sam. We take pride in your accomplishments. But Pap, he couldn't stand the shame of one of his own turning out better than he did. He thought it made him look bad, and other folks might have actually thought badly of him, too, because of it."

"Then how come people are upset by my readin' books now? Why would people these days want to take readin' *away* from kids? You had the opportunity to read real books, even in school. Seems like most of you adults have turned into

Pap Finns, not wanting us to learn anything much, except maybe how to add and subtract apples from oranges and read about building highways."

"We found out that most kids don't really like reading much, Sam, to be honest with you. We have had to find ways to teach them the skills they will need in life and work, that's about all we can do. We can't get them interested in *Huck Finn* enough to warrant spending so much time on it in school."

"I guess I'm just wondering what it used to be like in school, for you, Mr. Willson, as a student and as a teacher. Don't you think we could do a few less boring things in class? No offense to you, sir, and your teaching. But I don't know what I want to be yet. Maybe I'll work in the plant for Mr. Stevens, or maybe I'll be a college professor. Who says that isn't possible?"

"Well, the first answer is your test scores, Sam. You know that. If you don't score on the tests, then you don't become a college professor of any sort. Your eighth grade test is so important for so many reasons. You can score well on it, too, Son, if you'll just take it."

Ms. Sanders popped her head out of the front door, saving them both from the dead end they were driving into. "You boys come on in for dinner, now. Chicken's on, your favorite, Sam." Sam walked in the door ahead of Mr. Willson, who followed dutifully.

10 – BABY STEPS BACKWARDS

At dinner they ate quietly. Most of the time they spent biting and chewing and swallowing and smiling, and saying pleasantries like, "This is great chicken, Mom, thanks. How did you know I wanted chicken?" and "Wow, Ms. Sanders, this is the best chicken I've had in a long while."

"It's Betsy, please Pete."

"Yes, ma'am," Pete said, looking up, knowing he had bungled again, "I mean, Betsy."

Sam found this exchange a little disturbing, so he changed the topic.

"I gave a copy of *Romeo and Juliet* to Mr. Jones today. He said he'd read it."

Pete and Betsy looked up from their chicken and met eyes, then they lowered them again, along with their chicken. In unison, they picked up their napkins and made an initial sweep of their greasy faces. Sam kept right on eating, not looking up.

Betsy spoke first, "*Romeo and Juliet*? That's not really a book for children or for Mr. Jones, Sam. Where did you get it? Why did you do that?"

"Well, Ms. Belders let me have a copy from the library and Mr. Jones told me he hadn't read a book or seen a play in a while when we talked in the car on the way back to school, and so I gave it to him to read. I thought he might like it and he'll give it back, Mom. Mr. Jones won't lose it."

"I know he won't lose it, Son. But what use could he make of *Romeo and Juliet*? What good would it do him?"

"Well, I guess I thought he'd like the part in there about the families fighting and what it led up to, what with his daughter dating that guy over in Anniston, you know, and him not liking it much?"

"Where in the world did you hear about that, Son? Pete, what *are* you teaching these kids in schools these days?"

"I'm sorry, Betsy, but I didn't cover the dating habits of Mr. Jones' children when we were learning about participles the other day."

"Well, I guess I didn't bargain on you being fresh, what with the meal being so good and all…Anyway, what do the Montagues and the Capulets have to do with anything, Sam? Is that right, Pete, the Montagues and the Capulets?"

"That's right, Mom," Sam said sarcastically, flabbergasted that she felt like she had to get confirmation from Mr. Willson on the names, "The families continued their longstanding feud, now over the impending marriage, saying it would never happen, so instead of living apart, Romeo and Juliet decided to die together, in love til the end, but tragically, only in death. That's what Mr. Jones will get if he doesn't let her go a little bit, trust her a little, maybe even meet the guy."

"Well, Son, you just don't know what it's like to be the father of a beautiful young woman with the world all ahead of her and you having brought her all that way unscathed, or so you think," she shot back quickly. "I remember what it was like for *my* father to let me date *your* father. He could hardly stand it, you know. It just about killed him, especially that first night when Paul came over in that souped-up Chevy Nova he dug out of a junk heap and fixed up. It was a loud, and sassy car. That was your father, too, loud and sassy."

"Really? I never knew him to be loud and, sassy? What does that even mean, 'sassy'?" queried Sam.

"You didn't know him the way I did, and that's the way the Montagues and Capulets knew they didn't know Romeo and Juliet. So much at stake, so uncertain, and filled with prejudice. But people usually come around these days. My dad did, Sam. Mr. Jones will, I'd bet on it."

Mr. Willson watched and listened to this fascinating exchange. It reminded him of old television shows he used to watch and books he used to read where families sat around the dinner table and talked. But he hadn't had a literary conversation with a student or a colleague in so long that he had almost forgotten how to participate.

"More mashed potatoes, Pete?"

"Please, Betsy. Thank you," he said.

11 – GOOD NIGHT, SWEET PRINCE

They were so full from dinner that they could barely move, so they sat around the table talking, then finally each of them helped clean up and make the house look and feel "unlived in" again as soon as possible. Betsy liked to keep the house clean, to have things in order. They gathered by the front door to say their good-byes at about 8:30.

"So, Pete, what do you think we should do about Sam?"

Sam stood right there, a little embarrassed that his mother had asked Mr. Willson the question directly, and not him.

"Well, I think that's something that Sam needs to decide, really, Betsy. I mean, I know you are responsible for him. You are his mother, after all. But he's the one who has to make some decisions about what he's going to do. From what I understand, Dr. Dormont is committed to getting him to take the end of year test. There is so much riding on that exam for the school and for Sam. She's not going to let him get away with it, and she's probably going to pull him from my class and put him in cubicle 1 for the rest of the year to make sure that he is focusing on his work, preparing for the test, and not giving the other kids ideas about not studying, or heaven forbid, pulling what he pulled today and not taking the test at all."

"I hear you have some experience with students not taking the test at all."

Betsy's comment caught Pete off guard, and Sam's head swiveled back to Mr. Willson for his reply.

"Well, if you are talking about Paul, yes, that's right. But that's the only time in 24 years of teaching that I have done something like that. And it was the right thing to do. His future depended on it."

"Yes, well, this one's future depends on us, too, but you can't take the test for Sam these days. You'd get caught, and that wouldn't solve anything. Besides, that's just not right anyway."

"No, it wouldn't be. What do you think then? Better yet, what do you think, Sam?"

They turned their attention to him now.

"I'm not taking the test in June," he said.

"I know, honey, I know," Betsy said, as she took his head in her arms and kissed him softly on the forehead. "I know."

"I know, too," said Mr. Willson. "Goodnight to you both, and thank you for a wonderful evening."

"Goodnight."

"Goodnight."

Betsy closed the door behind them. They stood there inside the door, still hold-ing each other, listening to Mr. Willson's old truck rattle off, skidding stones back into the drive as he got back on the road. They smiled at that.

Betsy cupped Sam's head in her hands, kissed his forehead again and again, saying, as was her custom, "Good night, sweet prince."

"Goodnight, Mom."

"Now you go read, and I'll see you in the morning."

Sam practically hopped up the steps.

She watched him bound up, knowing he was becoming a man but not wanting him to do it so fast. She knew that they were in for a fight now, too, and though she wasn't completely won over to the idea of bucking the system, she loved her son and saw merit in his fight, at least to this point.

Betsy turned and looked out the front window one last time before going to bed herself, knowing she wouldn't see it, but hoping at least to hear the rumble of an old Chevy Nova coming up the drive. It never sounded, and she never slept.

12 – SCHOOL DAZE

The next day started the same as the day before. The test preparation routine became the mode for the school. There wouldn't be any runaway grocery store balls or long trips into town on bikes or contraband books changing hands. No, today would be like the next day and the next day to come until test day in early June. Dr. Dormont assigned Sam to cubicle 1, given a second chance by the district to conduct himself in a "pure and fruitful manner" for the rest of the year or risk suspension from school and the loss of his status as an eighth grader.

Dr. Dormont put this all in a formal letter that Sam and his mom had to sign. The agreement meant that Sam had to complete a minimum amount of work each day on the computer in preparation for the test or risk being expelled, which Betsy couldn't afford to have happen. She needed to work. She didn't have any way to afford staying home. Sam had to stay in school.

Sam complained to Mr. Willson and to his mother, but neither of them had any clout with the administration or the school board. Besides, the community didn't even know what to do with or think about people who purposefully made trouble. They all knew kids in school who weren't quite up to the work, who simply didn't have the capability for learning the material and getting the answers right on the tests no matter the drilling and training they received. These kids were just part of the school system like any other. But to have a kid who could score on the tests and wouldn't?

Sam wanted to be in class, no matter how boring. He missed his friends, and even his daily, although nearly deadly routine with Mr. Willson. Now his days consisted of getting to school, walking to his cubicle, turning on the computer, and completing reading and math drills on material he had mastered before. The computer kept track of his work, and timed his activities. He had to reach certain performance goals in certain time periods during each day. Time and again he read the same, worn out texts. One text was about shipping apples up the Hudson River: How long did it take for the ship to get from point x to point y if traveling at 20 knots? Was the driver of the ship the first mate or the captain? The next one was about ore mining and energy production: How many tons of ore does it take to produce x amount of energy? Where do the miners live during long shifts away from their families?

Every once in awhile, if he got ahead of the computer and had a little time, he would pull out Salinger's *Catcher in the Rye* from his bag and read a few pages. Sam brought the book into school illegally every day. Mr. Jones simply didn't check his bag like he did so many other kids' bags. The media center specialist, Ms. Hatcher, caught him with the book, and quizzed him over his shoulder about it; he hadn't noticed her there before she caught him with the book, having just encountered the first museum scene in the book and beginning to wonder along with Holden, "What happens to ducks in the winter when the lake ices over?" He had been captivated by Holden, losing track of the computer and of Ms. Hatcher.

"Well, here's our own little Holden Caulfield reading *Catcher*, ignoring the machine," her words startled Sam. "I suppose it's been 20 years or so since I read that," continued Ms. Hatcher, taking the book gently from him, turning it over and over, examining it like one might an everyday dish on an auction table, rather indifferently, focusing on the mundane.

"I haven't seen a copy in years. We have a really good part of the book on the computer, you know, Sam, with pictures and everything," she offered, warming up a little. "Why don't you use that, and put this old beat-up copy away? You know it's contraband?" She handed the book back to him.

Sam sensed a "half-asking" tone in her voice, an uneasiness in her, an opening like so many adults had been giving him lately.

"What's your favorite part of the book, Ms. Hatcher?"

"Hey, aren't you due for some math problems on your computer? I'm not going to contribute to your delinquency, smarty," she said turning away.

"No, I've done most of those, ma'am. Please, your favorite part?"

She wheeled around and marched back purposefully, almost angrily, and pulled the chair from the adjoining cubicle up close to Sam's.

"Sam," she said, pausing for effect, leading off her big speech. She never said much, but this had been boiling inside since she heard about what happened the day Sam missed the test, how the eighth graders came up just short of their target performances and the school lost money as a result, "You're killing us. The whole system is set up to run efficiently, to make your time here at school productive. We don't want you wasting your time reading books and such nonsense. We've got work to do here, can't you see that?"

"Your favorite part?"

Flabbergasted, she finally responded, "Well, to be honest, I don't remember much about the book. It was a long time ago, and I remember not really getting it when I read it the first time. But I do remember, now that you ask, after all these years, feeling like I understood what Holden meant by the word phoney, how he couldn't stand phoney people and phoney things. I can appreciate what it must feel like to be stuck in places where everything and everyone all around you is a sham," she caught herself, now looking into his eyes again, knowing that she had just admitted her complicity in his confinement, but he didn't let on. She was, she knew, a great, big phoney.

"Yeah, I liked that part, too, and the part about Ackley. Jerry Winston, in the seventh grade, is like Ackley, but I like him a lot anyway. He's real, and awful, but there's something about him that you can't pin down that you like a little bit, too, you know? I don't know," his voiced wondered off as he turned back to the computer, beckoning him back with its final warning beeps.

Ms. Hatcher watched him as he got started working again. The screen popped up with a series of 100 math questions, all of them multiplication and division operations, just numbers, more computation. Sam got to it, and as she looked over his shoulder she noticed that he steadily, quickly got all of the answers correct. He didn't miss any and had plenty of time to spare. When he finished, he took a deep breath, more like a sigh, and started in on the next set of operations, banking his time at the end of each set. The next set got a little harder, involving some algebra. But he could handle it.

At the end of that set, knowing that she remained behind him, watching, he turned to her and said, "Ms. Hatcher, if I get these all done and I have a little time left over, would you like to read from *Catcher* with me?"

She looked all around the media center, no one was there, as usual. She heard her watch ticking the time away slowly, like it did everyday in that lonely place. She looked at the door, too, and saw no movement in the hallways. She pondered another moment, and said, "Yes, Sam, I'll read with you," in a near whisper.

He turned back to his work, completing screen after screen on the computer. In the end, he had banked 12 minutes of free time. They read together through lunch.

13 – CLASS TIME

Mr. Willson addressed his class like he did every afternoon after lunch, except during this long month's stretch without Sam sitting in his regular seat. He barely saw Sam, only occasionally catching a glimpse of him through the window in the media center. Dr. Dormont basically closed off the media center to teachers and the general population of students. Only students with particular difficulties, like Sam, used that area of the school any longer.

So, Mr. Willson made his usual speech after lunch, outlining the afternoon's activities for the students, "Okay, class, I hope you all had a good, nutritious lunch. You're going to need the energy for the math pre-test. Three-hundered sample questions await your attention on your computer screens. During the next two hours, I'll be helping those of you who are having difficulties with solving simple equations. If you finish early and you have an acceptable performance rate – on these items the rate is 88% – then you may read quietly from your screens from the reading pre-test library. I found the pieces about leather-making and the Strategic Arms Limitation Treaty (SALT) talks in the 1970s to be very interesting among the choices for today. Enjoy those, and remember they will be on the test in June. The computer will buzz you in and will be tracking your scores. Let's do a good job on this set, class. Any questions? Go."

The students got right to the work. Most of them completed their problem sets quickly and read quietly at their terminals, but some of the students just couldn't seem to make much progress after a quick start. Several of them even slept, their heads nodding onto the terminals. This had happened before in Pete's classes, but it seemed to be happening more and more lately. It made Mr. Willson angry and sad and confused. The teaching approach the teachers used came to them so highly touted, guaranteeing them higher test scores. It had been working for years.

His students had been scoring at just about the same levels as they always had, with little blips of improvement among certain groups, but he began to see signs that improvement wouldn't continue. Students slept, students didn't perform on the assignments up to their capabilities, they asked to do other things in class. These things generally never happened before.

He knew the class bored the socks off his students and him. But he didn't see any other way of getting the students to perform on the tests. The curriculum had been determined by the state and handed to the teachers. The tests had been put in place, closely mirroring the curriculum in most cases. In order to get the school funds rightfully allotted to them, the teachers simply had to get the students to perform on the tests. If the students scored, the money flowed in. If they didn't, the state took over, brought in a new staff after firing the old teachers without recourse, and got it right themselves. Teachers had lost so much ground as a group over the years, but using this approach nearly insured that students would meet the standards and teachers would keep their jobs. He didn't like what he had become. But what would he be without teaching?

Pete moved around the room and helped a student here or there. The pace of the school day flowed during these moments, the only moments he had for interacting with the students anymore. The school programmed everything else during the day so that he had little opportunity to teach anything to the whole class or to individuals for that matter. He used to do some of this type of teaching back in the day, but now he basically had time only for reading directions to the drill sets the students were required to repeat each day at their screens. And before, when schools more loosely organized themselves, sometimes even around students' interests, he found himself battling students trying to figure out what to do, creating the curriculum with them as he taught.

But he had been thinking these last perilous days that Sam Sanders may have a point about the test and his class. Perhaps the test and everything else associated with it, including how the test dominated the flow of each day in school, kept people from learning. And he hardly even knew his students anymore. At least when he used to argue with them about doing their work and figuring out what to study, he got to know them, their personalities, what they liked, what made them tick. His students didn't really have the opportunity to get to know him, either. They got so busy with their coursework that they paid little attention to him. Or, they were sleeping.

After helping the last straggler to complete the problem set, Mr. Willson reached over on his desk for the copy of *Huck Finn* that Sam let him keep before. He began reading about the Duke and the Dauphin, the part he never got over when he read it as a kid. "How could people be so stupid?" he wondered. And then he wondered what he could possibly do about his class. "Maybe we've been duped, too," he mumbled out loud to himself.

The students overheard this comment and asked him what he meant.

"Nothing class, ignore me, and go back to work," he ordered. But he kept thinking. "Maybe tomorrow will hold something different for us."

14 – UNDERCOVER

When the final bell of the day sounded, Mr. Willson drained the last bit of coffee from his cup. The coffee had helped him make it through the afternoon activity, an on-line question and answer session with his class about the leather making industry. Deadly boring. He had reached a breaking point, and decided to do something about it.

After school, he walked quickly past Dr. Dormont's office without looking in and even faster toward the media center. He wished time didn't compress so much in school. He never had any time to talk to other teachers, their day had been scripted out so tediously and their work from each other so isolated. Better, the school thought, to avoid the problem of teachers sharing ideas regarding teaching and learning. This activity would just cloud their commitment to the curriculum and their test preparation regimen, like it did in the old days. After all, past exemplary test performances had brought an increase in technology resources, a new wing of computerized classrooms, and faculty bonuses.

He hoped to catch Ms. Hatcher, the media center specialist, before she left for the day.

The Duke and the Dauphin had done something to him, something that carried him all the way into the bright, beautiful, and lonely media center.

"Hello, Ms. Hatcher, how are you today? Where's Sam?" Pete asked as he entered the big empty room.

"Oh, Sam's on his way home, finished for the day. Does Mr. Sanders bring you down here, Mr. Willson, or something else?" she wondered.

Pete put his head down as close as possible to hers without making her uncomfortable. Talking to the ground, he asked, "Could we talk quietly in your office?"

"Why, of course, we can," she motioned him into her office, confused a bit, but curious about what could be going on. She didn't have spirited interactions like this in school much anymore. Now she'd had a whole day's worth.

They sat close to each other in the two chairs pushed along a small white table, the entire contents of her small office, except for a tall, white filing cabinet along the back wall. Mr. Willson began again.

"Harriet, I'm afraid I may be putting you in the middle of something you may not want to get into, but I need to ask you a favor. You say the word and I'll walk out of here and leave you alone. But you might be one of the only people I can trust, and I think you might be able to help me."

"Pete, I'm a little surprised by all this. You sound like you're *undercover* or something. What have you gotten yourself into? What do you want?"

"I'm going to teach *Huck Finn,* and not from the computer version. I want the books, Harriet, the books. Can you help me get them?"

Ms. Hatcher looked down at her hands, folded on the table. She paused a long time before answering. "Pete, I've been spending time with Sam here in the media center," she said, another long pause followed as she measured her words. "We talked about Holden Caulfield. I haven't thought about Salinger in years. And then we read from the book together. I didn't get anything else done today. We've been talking and thinking about it all day long. Do you realize what will happen if you do this? This is far outside the parameters laid down for the curriculum. I'm sure you haven't asked Dr. Dormont for permission to do it, especially with the test coming up in a few weeks. What are you thinking?"

"I'm thinking that I'd like to be a teacher again. I remember doing this sort of thing when I first started out years ago. I've given my life over to this boring curriculum and these tests, and where has it gotten us? We have one Sam Sanders, and we have very little to do with that even. I don't know my students. Maybe some of them would be interested in stories, ideas, life itself, for that matter, if we did something in school with all of this time besides drills on the computer."

"Yes, well, that's a nice speech and all, but you would be taking a huge risk, and I would be taking a huge risk, too. You can't possibly get away with it. You'll be found out soon enough, even if you try to hide it. And people will know where you got the books."

"So you do know where they are?" a glimmer came back to Pete's eyes again. "You know, Harriet, maybe I want to be found out."

"Why?"

"I can't go on like this, Harriet. I've been throwing my life and my students' lives away by saying nothing, just doing what I'm told to do, forsaking gifts I have to share with people to serve a system I don't and can't believe in anymore."

Harriet took a deep breath, and held it, and let it out long and slow, contemplating.

Then suddenly she said, "Meet me back here at 7:30 tonight."

"Thanks, Harriet," he touched her hand in gratitude to seal the deal. "You do know where the books are then?"

"7:30," was all she said as she got up to close the center down for the day.

Pete walked out, not looking back. Harriet watched him leave, then took a look around the palace of technology that she had grown to hate with a passion. She pulled out the lone drawer in her table, and reached way back, and pulled out a set of old keys.

"Here we go," she said to herself, closing the drawer and closing the book on a period in her professional life she'd like to lock away forever.

15 – THE TREASURE TROVE

It's hard to keep a truck like Willson's quiet, especially when you really want to. Pete pulled into the school parking lot a little bit before 7:30, and the truck backfired as he pulled into the lot, "Infernal combustion engines!" he muttered under his breath. Other expenses kept him from getting one of the newer, more efficient battery-powered cars like most of the other teachers had. He continued to pour gasoline into his car long after most of his friends had little idea of where to even get the strange smelling, flammable liquid. The car remained an asset to him as a result; the truck made him a bit unique, even eccentric to some. Pete didn't mind that at all.

Mr. Willson entered the school through the main entrance. He had no choice, the main entrance being the only one accessible to faculty after hours. The cameras no doubt caught his image as he entered, no way to avoid them. He would have to explain to Dr. Dormont why he came back to school. She would have seen his face in the nightly security report the next day. He rehearsed an answer in his head, though he had always been a terrible liar.

"I had to come back and get my jacket," was the best thing he could come up with.

He wondered if he could possibly sound sincere, even with a simple answer, though he really had left his jacket at school that day.

The trickiest part would be explaining to Dr. Dormont why the camera shot him going to the media center and then meeting with Ms. Hatcher. He had no idea where Harriet would be taking him after they met, but he had the feeling that Dr. Dormont would know about this very soon, every move. In schools these days, the need for security outweighed any reasonable commitment to privacy. Cameras hung everywhere. His mind flitted around a hundred other alibis.

Pete thought about the risk he had taken asking Harriet about helping him find the books. He had heard once that a few people in the school knew where the old book sets for instruction were kept, but he never asked about them or saw them. He figured most of the people who knew the story had retired by now. He sort of expected that Harriet would refer him to somebody else, and maybe give him a history lesson on the topic. He never expected her to actually know who could find the books.

Ms. Hatcher met him just inside the media center doors.

"Pete," she whispered, "the cameras are turned off in here. I was able to disengage them for 30 minutes. I'm supposed to clean them and restock the discs in them every week, so this turns out just right, but we have to hurry. Follow me."

He followed her. Her breathy voice and stealth-like movements made him feel like a criminal.

In her office, Harriet pushed her filing cabinet to the side, then she took out a set of keys. One of the keys worked in a white door that stood semi-hidden where the filing cabinet usually stood. Strange, Pete had never noticed a door there before. The door blended in with the wall. It had no door knob, only a keyhole. Harriet opened it to a wooden staircase that went way down two floors.

They hurried down together, and at the foot of the stairs there remained one last steel door.

"This is it," she said as she fumbled with the keys. As she placed several wrong keys in the hole over the course of several seconds, which seemed more like endless minutes to Pete, he noticed a light under the door. He also noticed Harriet's hands shaking.

"Harriet, do you see that light?" he whispered, "Is that usually there? Are you okay?"

She moved her head down slowly, soaking up the light and then looking up to meet his eyes squarely. Fear buried itself deep inside her now.

Ms. Hatcher stepped back. Pete held her arm, steadied her.

"Harriet?"

"Pete, I've never seen a light inside that room from the *outside*. Somebody is in there."

"Just think of it this way, Harriet. Whoever is in there must be a friend, right?"

Her mind raced as she pondered this possibility. She stepped back to the door, and found the right key, turning the lock, saying, "Here goes nothing." She had courage, and Pete admired her for it.

"Or," Pete added, "Here goes everything."

They opened the door and walked inside the room. The room measured approximately 60' wide by 80' long by 12' high. Huge. Shelves covered each wall from floor to ceiling. Each inch of each shelf contained books, with covers, and pages, and lives. Other free-standing bookcases filled in the room, all standing around a desk in the center of the room.

This sight awed them both. But more incredible, a lone person sat in an easy chair at the big desk in the middle of the room, reading, and smoking. They could only see the person's head from behind. The person had what appeared to be some sort of old earphone device covering his or her ears. And the person moved in the seat, like a dancer.

Pete and Harriet, now holding hands, moved slowly around the desk and into the sight line of the reader. At first they startled the reader. But once they recognized each other, they stood there merely confused. Not frightened, but very, very confused.

"Dr. Dormont?"

16 – AS CLEAR AS...?

"Well," said Dr. Dormont, removing the earphones once her eyes met theirs, "Ms. Hatcher, Mr. Willson? To what twist of fortune or fate do I owe your visit here tonight?"

"First things first," Pete offered back, feeling a fleeting sense of the upper hand, "That looks like one of those pocket cd players we used to take from the kids. I haven't seen one of those in years. I didn't even know you could get batteries for them anymore. By the way, what are you doing down here?"

"There are a lot of things you don't know about me, Mr. Willson," offered Dr. Dormont, as she took a last drag on her cigarette and stamped it out in the ashtray on the desk, filled with many, many other butts. "Like the fact that I read books a lot, and come down here often. Harriet knew about the room because I showed it to her and gave her a key a long time ago, just in case. She's never seen me down here. She never knew about the second entrance. But she knows the story. I'm the architect of this stash. The School Board wanted to 'dispose' of all of these books when everything students read in the curriculum went on-line and when we remodeled the media center, but we argued against just trashing the books, especially against burning them, which some of our more illustrious citizens wanted to do. The board gave us one weekend back in 2006 to do something with them. This is what we came up with, converting the old fall out shelter. Only a few of us know about the books. We just felt like at any time the tide could turn and even reading could be outlawed. We wanted to preserve what we had."

"Who is 'us' and 'we' and how come I didn't know about it?" quizzed Pete.

"You were too young back then, just starting out in teaching, remember?" continued Dr. Dormont. "I didn't want to put you in jeopardy that early in your career. Besides I had plenty of friends in the English Department and plenty of friends in town who could keep a secret and who could work a saw or a hammer."

"But why hide the books? Why not give them to the library, or hand them out to people who could use them?"

"Good questions, Pete, I'm glad to see that these 20 years in teaching haven't completely deadened your inquiry skills," commented Dr. Dormont, as she leaned back in her seat now more comfortably. She looked as if she were sitting in her principal's chair in her office, except she was surrounded by thousands of books.

"The truth is that nobody wanted the books. We asked around. The library didn't want whole sets of the same books when they already had multiple copies of many of the titles. No other institution wanted them, either. They just didn't have room or thought that books would become dispensible, which they largely have," she went on with the story.

"Some of us thought that books might make a comeback someday, that maybe this whole technology thing might lose some steam. But technology just kept moving, and the test made it impossible to use books anymore."

"I want to use them, Dr. Dormont, that's why we're here," Pete offered.

"Mr. Willson, exactly how stupid do you think I am?"

"Stupid enough, or crazy enough, depending on how you look at it, to keep thousands of basically contraband books locked up in a cellar only a few living people know about, and stupid enough to get caught down here reading and smoking and listening to classic rock while two amateurs figure the whole thing out. It's like you wanted to get caught. You don't think I'm crazy any more than I think you're crazy, though I do think this is all very strange, don't you?"

Silence fell on them while Dr. Dormont pondered Pete's words. Harriet and Pete awaited her reply. Dr. Dormont lit another cigarette.

"Let me tell you where I am now, Mr. Willson. Sam Sanders has gotten to me. This kid is reading, all of the time, and he's asking questions, making statements. He's brave, and bold, and I think he's a beautiful kid. We used to see boys and girls like him all the time at Downing, but I haven't seen a 'Sam Sanders'-type kid in 15 years. However," she paused here again, taking a drag on her cigarette and considering her answer carefully, "we have so few teachers who would even know what we are talking about if we asked them to teach from a real book in class. So many have never read a book all the way through or even held one, it's just not a part of teacher training anymore, let alone a norm in most college programs of any kind. And whom do you know who can conduct a class discussion? We haven't done that in years. And if we started using books again, what would become of our test scores? How would we compete for funds with surrounding districts? How could we change the minds of our constituents, especially our parents, who think we are doing a good job now? We would lose funding, and jobs. Pete, I can't afford to lose my job at the end. You know how much is riding on these last two years of my contract. I'll be able to retire at 40 years of service. There's nothing for me after 38 years; I'll lose everything."

Pete listened dutifully, taking in again all the reasons he already knew for why he couldn't go back to books and teaching the way he used to teach. He respected Dr. Dormont. She hired him right out of college, and since then always treated him with respect. But he felt her reach had been shortened, cut off by the politics of the job, and by a lack of will to fight for what she believed in, what she thought to be right and sound educationally for the school and for society. He was just now finding his will, after all these years. He prepared to make his stand, make one last argument.

17 – SONGS IN THE NIGHT

"Listen, Dr. Dormont, I don't profess to know everything that is in your head and heart. After all, this is the first I've heard about of all this, and these books have been down here for 22 years. But what I do know about you is that you have always supported teachers when you thought their efforts would help students. Sam is showing us that what we do everyday isn't working for some of our students, certainly not for him. And I know that I could do a better job in the classroom if the curriculum and the test didn't dictate every move I make. They just hang out there over our heads, unchallenged. They are driving us and we have had literally no say in what they are. We serve them like masters, instead of creating them ourselves and making them work toward our devices, our ends. Long ago, teachers used to talk about protecting and nurturing their profession. But we don't have a profession anymore. Instead, we act like mechanics, keeping a well-oiled machine running. Sure it runs smoothly most of the time, but what does it do for us, for our students? Produce mediocre test scores? Basically. Help us learn to think and learn more, get interested in the world? Follow an interest, concern, or passion with fellow students and teachers to a productive end? I don't think any of these things happen much anymore, hardly anywhere. I used to think these things made for an education. Now they have almost disappeared as possibilities. They have all but disappeared from my teaching. What we have left is schooling, but in the most basic, mundane, and meaningless of school programs. Is this all we want? Is this all we can have? Why can't we get back to educating?"

Dr. Dormont stared at Pete, then moved her steely eyes over to Harriet's, and then back to Pete's. None of them moved, immobilized by the realization that years of actions in the school hadn't come close to meeting their dreams and goals. Her cigarette burning down, Dr. Dormont finally moved slowly over the table – putting her last cigarette out in the ash tray – and leaned back in her chair while Pete and Harriet stood as uncomfortably as ever.

"Persuasive. On the point, Pete. But I'm the choir, preacher. Tell me now, what are you going to actually *do* about the problem?"

"I'm going to teach *Huck Finn* for the last month of school. I don't care what it costs. I want to do something worthwhile with my students these last days of the year. If they want to take the test at the end of the year, fine. The school requires it and we expect them to take it. But I'm not going to encourage them about it or even mention it these last weeks. I know that Sam Sanders will not take the test. None of us can convince him to take it. But just sitting in the cubicle working on meaning-less, decontextualized skill drills? That isn't fair to him. And I want you to support me, Dr. Dormont, and even help me run interference with the community on this. I don't care how you bill it, as a sort of "Back to the Future" experiment or a trial run for a burned out teacher, but I need you to be behind me. Can you do it?"

This time, without a moment's hesitation, Dr. Dormont got up from her chair and walked over to the far wall. She looked up and pointed, saying, "I think there are 30 copies of *Huck Finn* on that fifth shelf, Pete. That ought to do it."

"Thank you, Dr. Dormont."

"It's Cindy, Pete."

"Thanks, Cindy."

After an awkward moment or two, Harriet chimed in, "I'll have to get some of those bindings tended before you pass the books out, Pete. They're a little loose, we don't want to lose the pages. I'll have them ready by tomorrow for you."

"Thanks, Harriet," Pete said calmly, as they loaded the books into a box and carried them up and out of the cellar into the light of the school. Night had fallen deeply now, and the school remained silent. Then Dormont made her last tour of the room as she always knew it, full of books and of forgotten potential. This would all change soon enough. She knew it.

18 – NEXT DAYS

Mr. Willson stayed up all that night re-reading *Huck Finn*. He planned on reading the first chapter out loud with the students the next day in class, and giving them a dose of background material that would help them situate Twain in the figurative pantheon of great American writers and the story in the historical period from which it sprang. After all this planning and no sleep, Mr. Willson felt strangely energetic, more so than usual when facing the students with the routine of a computer screen and sets of skill drills staring him and his charges in the face. He even felt bright-eyed when the students came into class. He felt even better when he saw Sam Sanders mixing back in among the first period class. Mr. Jones had delivered him from cubicle 1, mercifully freed by Dr. Dormont.

The students continued to file into the classroom in an orderly fashion, as usual. What they found inside the room looked outside the norm, though. Each of them had a copy of *Huck Finn* placed neatly on the desk with a blank journal and pen attached for writing responses to the book and to class discussions. Most of the students had seen books before, usually when they were in the lower grades and especially during preschool or at home. But most never read out of books anymore since most literature, in some format, could be found online at home or at school. Most of them hadn't written on paper with pens for years. A few of them had written thank you notes to their mothers as a tribute for Mother's Day during a history class activity in 4th grade.

Rather nervously, Mr. Willson answered the same rounds of questions with all of his classes at the beginning of each period. This made it hard to get into the lesson, but he vaguely remembered how crucial this type of warm-up was for learning. It had simply been a long time since he had allowed for student voices to exist in his classroom. He had to get back into practice.

The students wanted to know what was going on, how they would use the materials, what would be expected of them, how this would affect their preparation for the test. Many of them shared stories about how they used to read books, the last book they read, where their family members kept special copies of favorite books in the house and sometimes read from at family events. He and the class even laughed out loud at several of the funny stories, like the time that Jerome Whitsell kept trying to hide his sister Murphy's copy of *Charlotte's Web,* and no matter where he hid it Murphy would find it. And they caught a collective lump in their throats at some of the sadder stories, like the one Jenny Barstow told about coming home to find that her mom had literally trashed her entire series of Patsy Watson books.

"I loved those books," she said, holding a copy of *Huck Finn* close, pretending, no doubt, like it was her favorite Patsy Watson story *The Penguin's Missing Diamonds,* "and my mom just threw them out without even asking me. She said that books like that wouldn't help me get ready for the test, for life. I never really forgave her for that. I didn't know how to argue with her then, how to tell her how I felt about those books and what she had done to me."

Pete felt somewhat surpised by the students' willingness to speak up in class since they had little opportunity in school to do so, most of the time. But he felt glad for their courage and willingness, and it added so much to the class hour, which flew by.

Overall, the day proved to be outstanding. No class made it through reading chapter one completely, but they all seemed eager to continue. Mr. Willson had to spend extra time explaining how writing in their journals would enhance their understanding of the book and of themselves, all new ground for them. The students had gotten used to reading stories for the facts of the matter, not for ideas or for how they related to the story, let alone how the story made them feel. They had almost no experience of reading an entire book.

As he walked out of the building at the end of the day, feeling exhausted in a way he hadn't felt for 20 years, Mr. Willson stopped by the teacher's room to pick up a cup of coffee for the short ride home, but more to keep him going for the reading and the writing that lay ahead of him in preparation for the next day's classes. He had no idea that what happened inside his classroom would be attacked from the outside. It had been 20 years since he had been involved in any type of campus politics. Things were changing rapidly, however, inside his class, and inside the school.

19 – HOT COFFEE

As he entered the teacher's room to get his cup of hot coffee on the way out, Pete noticed a group of teachers standing, whispering by the coffee machine, and they stopped talking, suspiciously, when he came in.

He couldn't help noticing this, since it had never happened before, and after all, among the group were his friends Teddy Hersh and Marcia Tolkens.

"Hey, what's up? What's the big secret?" Pete asked the group, hoping to be let in on the story as he plopped bills into the machine.

"Well, not much," replied Teddy, "except that we all know about what you're doing and can't believe that you are doing it. Setting us back 20 years, just like that. We have been doing so well, too, Pete. Why would anyone in their right mind pull a stunt like this? Teaching from a book, for heaven's sake, with just a few weeks of school left to go til the biggest test of the students' academic lives and of our fiscal year? What are you doing?"

A bombshell is a bombshell. He hadn't spoken to Teddy or anyone else in the group for years about teaching. Most of their conversations were about the coffee machine not working quite right and pay scales for teachers in other districts (which were usually higher). Pete pulled his coffee cup out of the dispenser, and turned to the group, stirring some cream into the cup.

"Well, Teddy, Marcia, Henry, Lois," he addressed them all by name, "I'm teaching again. Dr. Dormont and I decided it would be all right to give *Huck Finn* a try here at the end of the year. Sam Sanders had a lot to do with that, what with his reading and all, inspiring me, really, to go back to some of the things that I think could make my classroom a place for learning again, and not just a place for test preparation."

"Nice, real nice," Teddy replied, still put out and sarcastic, "so you're teaching *again*, are you? What does that make what we're doing, then? And what is Dormont's motive for supporting this?" she asked, now seething.

"No need to get angry, Teddy. Dr. Dormont opened up the basement below the media center, where all of the school's books had been stored for 20 years. I bet you didn't know that. I didn't know it until last night, and she's making plans to move some of the books back into the media center. She's going to encourage all of us to use the books, however we see fit in the coming weeks and next year. It's really up to us, Teddy, what we decide to do. But she's decided to help us any way we see fit, even so far as taking the hits for us if our test scores fall."

"You don't get it, do you, Pete? Some of us have invested a lot in this process. Some of us think this might be the highest scoring eighth grade class ever. Do you realize what gets thrown out if we don't nurture that potential, focus in on helping them reach the highest achievement scores that they can? We lose the financial package for schools that comes with scores in the state's top 10 as well as the bonus package for teachers that we've never gotten before. Some of us were counting on that, Pete. We've played this game fairly, humanely. Our students are well-adjusted and smart. They can compete for these resources as well as any class in the state. And now you want to start talking about ideas and learning and teaching? These are the things we escaped from 20 years ago. Don't you remember the long days, the uncooperative students, the relentless stream of papers to grade, the endless preparation and the load of reading? That's all gone now and you want to bring it all back? Having the kids write in a journal? Who's going to read their journals, Pete? You. That's right. You're going to read them. Not me," and Teddy stomped out of the room, followed by the others.

At least Marcia shrugged her shoulders apologetically to Pete as she chased after Teddy. But they all left Pete standing there alone. He had a sinking feeling that this wouldn't be the last time in the coming days for that feeling. He leaned back against the coffee machine and thought to himself, "Well, the other option is silence. And I know where that has gotten us. I guess it's time for everybody to make a speech." He left the building, and headed for home, trying hard not to let the coffee room event cloud the concentration he needed for teaching chapter two of *Huck Finn.* He had truly entered uncharted waters.

20 – QUESTIONS…AND ANSWERS

Mr. Willson never anticipated the type of excitement that *Huck Finn* would generate in his classes. He thought he'd get excited about it, but hadn't anticipated that his students would follow suit. In the past 20 years, no assignment or project had ever caught his students' attention the way this one had. He felt like he should be making more progress with the lessons he had planned each day, but he realized that he really didn't want to contain the students. Instead, he allowed his instincts to guide him more than the plans he made, encouraging the students to ask questions and to talk to each other about possible answers to their questions, and more questions. He realized that this approach caused him to have to be even more prepared for each lesson.

The students wrote each day in their journals, sometimes to prompts he gave about the reading or class discussion. Sometimes he left it up to students to write about what they were determined to focus on. Some of the students asked to take the books and their journals home with them at night. Mary Polleck asked, "I guess I'm just wondering why Huck and Jim don't just ditch the raft on the east side of the river and make their way back to Cairo and head for the east, or north toward freedom. Why keep going down the river? They can get off that raft anytime they want."

Bill added, "Yeah, Mr. Willson, don't you think this is a whole lot of writing to get to the point? What is the point, anyway?"

Pete just shrugged his shoulders and looked at the class.

Sam chimed in, "Well, the way I see it, Twain needed the time and the distance to tell his story. He hadn't gotten done with what he wanted to say yet. He needed the journey on the river south to confront more issues, more people, more events. That's the way I see it. The reader is in for the journey, all the way, right along with Twain, no matter how wild it gets. If he or she wants to get off the raft, then Twain hasn't done his job holding the reader."

Silence. Mr. Willson waited for a response. No one said anything else. He finally asked the students a question, "If we can accept Sam's notion of the journey, what do you think Twain wants us to learn so far from Huck and Jim's experiences?" He waited a few moments for the students to let the question sink in, then he prompted them to attempt an answer on their own, first, in their journals. The students began writing. Mr. Willson waited about 10 minutes, then began asking students all around the room to share their writing and their answers. Some did, some didn't. Some read their answers, and some just spoke extemporaneously based on what they had written. Some felt too shy or not yet finished enough to contribute. He said, "Okay," when they passed their turn, but promised that he would come back to them.

Dr. Dormont stuck her head in the door at the end of the period, and asked Mr. Willson for a few minutes of his time in the hallway. When the bell rang, Mr. Willson joined her and all the other students in the hallway. Amid the bustle and loud talking, no one else could hear their conversation.

"Dr. Dormont, to what do I owe this unexpected visit?" he asked her, nearly glowing from the class and wanting to tell her all about it.

"Pete, I know things are going well. The students are talking, loving the book. But a lot of the teachers are angry. The students are saying they don't want to work on their test-prep curriculum, they'd rather read. Some are actually reading copies of *Huck Finn* in their math classes. Some teachers asked for a faculty meeting to address this, and I've already gotten questions from concerned parents, both inside and outside of your classes, and the superintendent. School Board members, especially Mr. Stevens, want to know what's going on. It's coming quicker than I thought it would. You need to be at the faculty meeting after school tomorrow, and the board meeting in a few weeks. I just wanted you to know first-hand what's happening."

"Thanks, Cindy, I appreciate it. I guess I'm having too much fun to see that this is going to get harder faster. Don't pinch me anymore today, though. Leave me alone to enjoy this a little longer, in case it goes away just as fast as it came."

"I'll keep you posted, Pete, *tomorrow then.*"

"Right, tomorrow," and in the next breath he turned and shouted out to his gathering class, "take out your copies of *Huck Finn* and turn to…" and his voice drifted back behind closed doors.

Dr. Dormont listened for a moment and watched through the glass pane in the door as the class moved into the lesson, and she wished she could be teaching again, too. But her work for the day, and a career, had just begun. If the possibility of Pete continuing to teach existed much past the next day's events, much depended on her. She went back to her office and the phones.

21 – LIVING DEMOCRACY

The next day buzzed. The students understood that their class and their teacher were at the center of a fledgling controversy. Some of the students had put themselves and some of their other teachers at the center of the controversy as well, as the students periodically refused to do their in-class work and insisted on reading books instead. This did not sit well with many of the teachers, some of whom had never even read a book. The younger teachers, especially, found the whole situation to be so disturbing that one of the new teachers had marched into Dr. Dormont's office during second period to resign his position. He left the school immediately after telling Dr. Dormont, "This is the most unprofessional situation I could ever find myself in. This isn't teaching, this is babysitting now. I didn't come here to do this. I'm out of here."

As he left without fanfare, Dr. Dormont did not argue with him, or beg him to stay. The other teachers covered his open classes as best they could that day.

And so the building leaked and seethed at every point. People disagreed at the coffee machine in the teachers' lounge about what the purpose of schooling was and is, and how teaching and curriculum play a vital part in the process of schooling and education. On the phone, Dr. Dormont called back hysterical parents who threatened to remove their children from school and send them to a competing school just before the test. Then when things had almost settled down, Mr. Stevens barged into her office, hat in hand.

"Dr. Dormont, as a member of the school board, I'm here to register my formal complaint with you regarding what you are letting go on here. I know all about this Sam Sanders. You know, his dad used to work for me? Caused quite a stir before he died, trying to get me to put in a library in the employee lounge at the plant for the workers. But I held off that distraction. Soon as you know it, workers would be asking for higher wages and better health care packages, or unionizing. I know the type, so I stopped him, and then, well, you know, he's gone, so that got put to rest. But now here's this little Sam Sanders getting his teacher to teach a book, for heaven's sakes, and subsequently infecting our school. Right before the test? How could you let this go on, Dr. Dormont? How could a little truant cause so many problems? What are you thinking?"

"I guess that's just it, Mr. Stevens. I'm thinking again, thinking that what we've been doing in school lacks life and intellectual rigor. I'm trying to put those things back in, one step at a time. And I'm looking for teachers who are made for the project to stay on. I'm calling it 'Project Huck Finn.' We're going on a journey to find teaching and learning again. I think we can do it, and I don't think our test scores will suffer, either. Our kids will still be smart."

"I have never in all my days heard of such a thing. This will be the end of you here, I promise it," he threatened, before he walked out.

At the end of the school day, Mr. Willson poked his head into Dr. Dormont's office, "Hey, you comin' to the meeting, or what? You're running the thing. I think we're late already."

"I am not running the meeting, Pete. Teddy Hersh wanted the meeting, so I told her to call it and run it. I'm on the sidelines. I'll speak if I need to, but we have to see where the faculty is on this. I can't just push my agenda through, especially if there is no will for it on the part of the teachers. So we'll see what happens...Okay, you're right, let's go."

They walked out together and down the long hallway to the auditorium. The room already teemed with teachers. They respectfully made a path for Dr. Dormont and Pete all the way to the front. Dr. Dormont followed the opening to the front row and sat down, not taking the stage to call the meeting to order. She nodded to Teddy to take charge, which she did.

"Okay, everyone, please find a seat," Teddy directed from the lectern. "Can everyone hear me in the back, okay? Test? Test?"

A chorus of "yes's" trickled in from the gathered mass of about 40 teachers, and Teddy waited for collective calm.

Finally she spoke, "Thanks for gathering here today. I called this meeting of the entire faculty so that we could discuss what is going on with Mr. Willson's class, especially with his use of a class text outside the computer library of approved texts, and the sudden influx of student behavior problems related to this event. I also want to bring up the issue of Dr. Dormont's new initiative, 'Project Huck Finn,' which she described to all of us in executive summary on electronic mail today. I just want to say that I'm opposed to both of these developments. I've been teaching here 12 years, and I have enjoyed my work here. The students are compliant and smart, and they score well on the tests. I have been happy with our contract and I like living here. I want to stay. But these developments change everything, and I want you to know that they vary from my ideas of what good teaching truly is. I hope that by the end of the meeting I can make a formal motion that we as a faculty vote to suppress these two developments and get back to our jobs, that is, getting our students ready for the June tests, now just two weeks away. We all know how much is riding on those tests. This is no time to mess up what we have spent years and careers building. Thank you."

Teddy's remarks met with a smattering of applause. Everyone waited for the next speaker to rise and take the podium. No one had set an order for speakers, so the microphone remained open. Everyone expected that Dr. Dormont or Pete Willson would stand next. They were wrong.

After a few moments, instead, Stephany Bellweather arose and made her way slowly to the podium. She had her 75th birthday party at the school just two weeks before, thrown by the faculty as a whole in her honor. Everyone expected this to be her last year, her 50th year teaching math at the school. She fumbled around with the microphone before Mr. Pelters got the height of it right for her. Her voice crackled, but held firm throughout her short address.

"I'm not good at speeches, like Teddy Hersh," she laughed, "But I've got nothing to lose now, after losing so much over the last 30 years." The audience fell completely silent.

"I was here when we decided to teach the way we do now. Everyone, except a few of us, thought it was a good idea back then to throw all of our energy and know-how into the tests. It seemed practical to so many, so level-headed. Those of us in the minority went along, and adapted over time," she took a moment to wipe her brow with a handkerchief and to take a drink of water before going on.

"I was a member of the building crew who saved the books that still live under the school. I was proud of that accomplishment, but in the rush toward retirement, I've spent these last 30 years behind a computer, and barely in front of kids. I had almost forgotten about the books, too. I haven't thought about them or seen them in years. And I almost forgot what it was like to teach until I heard my students telling me stories these last days about their classes with Mr. Willson. I admire him for his courage, and Dr. Dormont as well. I just want you all to know that I won't be teaching the test preparation curriculum these last few weeks. Instead, I'm going to pull out some of the old science fiction that we stuck in the cellar, and help the students make contemporary connections between those stories and the development of new science today. That's what I'm doing, even if they fire me before I'm through. It's a very small sacrifice to make after giving everything else up these past 30 years. And I'd like to really teach before I retire, just one last time."

She walked away without any formal closing, and hugged Dr. Dormont and Pete Willson, while some members of the faculty applauded her. She made her way back to her seat to listen to those who would follow her, a tough act.

Other impassioned pleas followed. Faculty members appeared divided about what they should be doing. Many of them voiced concerns about the timing of the changes, wondering if it were wise to make changes when the students faced their most important school event, the test, in early June.

When everyone who wanted to do so had made his or her way to the microphone, Dr. Dormont finally took her turn, to close the meeting. Pete remained silent during the entire meeting, choosing to listen.

"I truly want to thank everyone for coming today and for speaking your minds. That's a tradition that has lasted here in this school, despite the fact that we haven't really had much to talk about for 20 years. I liked how you talked about teaching and learning, with care, and depth of thought. I want to make a suggestion that follows what I perceive to be a rather divided feeling on most of these matters, and there are certainly more than two polarized views. I'd like to suggest that we all agree to allow individuals or small teams of teachers to make their own decisions about curriculum and their teaching approach these last few weeks. Then, let's have a meeting after school is out, once we know our test scores, and then let's decide what we are going to do together, collectively, about this for next year. Is there a sense of agreement, or consensus, that this is a good idea?"

Dr. Dormont looked immediately at Teddy Hersh, who nodded her consent.

"Would anyone else like to speak to my point?"

Silence.

"Then we are agreed. We will reconvene here on June 13, our teacher work-day on the Monday after the Friday June 10 test, to discuss next steps together. Meeting adjourned."

The faculty milled around and talked. Teddy and Pete shook hands. Pete got Teddy a cup of coffee and they talked together, really for the first time in a very long time.

22 – THE NIGHT BEFORE

Up til now, I've mostly stayed out of the story, best I could. What follows is my more personal account of what happened at the end of the school year. I actually witnessed most of what I tell about in the remaining chapters.

The state's eighth grade test would be given on June 10, a Friday, at Downing School – the math portion in the morning, the language arts portion in the afternoon. All around the area, schools reported their strategies for test success to newspaper reporters, who tracked the school stories like they do candidates' stories during election season. Public relations staffers in the schools spin their stories, trying to make their schools look the best they can. They highlight the exceptional, focused efforts of everyone attempting to raise test scores. They set up "boiler rooms," where volunteers and staffers constantly work the phones day and night, calling constituents to drum up support and seeking donations to make the event successful. They set up special meals for students and staffers and for last-minute community volunteers to tutor students "on the bubble" of passing, even into the night before the test.

Having covered the spring testing season many times, I noticed the wire had little to say about Downing and its district's effort. Downing's staff usually hit the media airwaves hard, pumping up the district's efforts in order to cast them in the best light. They usually sent flyers, and electronic messages, and published their own testing newsletters. Yet nothing had come to me from them this year. I had been so busy, I guess, that I hadn't really noticed the gap until just then. I decided to attend the "Night Before Gala," sponsored each year by the school board.

I called the school to get some last minute details.

"Good morning, this is Missy Tallons from the *Record-Star*. How are you today?"

"Fine," said Ms. Burton, the school secretary.

"Terrific. I'm just looking for some information about the 'Night Before Gala,' I've attended it for several years running now, but I haven't heard anything about it this year. Is it still on for tonight?"

"Yes, well, we'll be having our usual Thursday night board meeting, nothing special. It is a public meeting, of course, so you are welcome to come."

I sensed Ms. Burton was leaving a lot out.

"If you don't mind me saying, Ms. Burton, this is awfully strange, really. Downing always does so well on the tests and is always so public about its test preparations. It just seems odd for you not to be having the Gala and to have heard nothing from you these past few weeks," I quizzed.

"Yes, you are welcome to come to the board meeting tonight. It begins at 7 p.m."

"Okay then, thank you, Ms. Burton. You're sure there isn't something else?"

"No, Ms. Tallons. Goodbye," Ms. Burton offered nothing more.

"Goodbye, then, Ms. Burton…"

"How strange," I thought, "I wonder what is going on out there?"

I left early to be sure to get to Downing a little before 7 pm in order to get a good seat, and perhaps to talk to a few people, maybe the school board members and the superintendent, and one of my school favorites, Dr. Cindy Dormont, before the meeting got started.

When I finally drove into the parking lot, I couldn't find a space to park. Traffic had been backed up for about a mile from the school and had caused a considerable delay. I glanced down at my watch, 6:55 pm. While on the road waiting, I thought the delay might have been caused by a stalled truck, a piece of farm equipment or an accident, the typical things that delayed you in a small town, or out in the country. But it was the pure volume of cars causing the delay. The custodial and security staffs patrolled the parking lots directing people to park on the athletic fields surrounding the school. I hadn't seen a crowd like this for a school event, athletic or academic, during my entire reporting career. People came teeming from the town and surrounding areas, they unloaded their cars, and streamed for the doors. What could be happening?

I had to walk a half-mile just to get back to the school from my parking place on the outfield of the baseball field. Once inside the school, I found myself locked out of the board meeting, which had been moved from the boardroom at the school – a comfortable, small venue – to the gymnasium. The gym held 1,675 people at maximum occupancy, according to the fire code poster hanging near the doorway. I remember jotting this fact down in my notebook, noting officially one sign among many that a big story brewed.

The school staff had set-up closed-circuit TV monitors for the overflow crowd. I finally landed in the media center. Ms. Hatcher tuned the TV to public access channel 17 for the crowd now packing itself in to the center's limits. We would be at capacity soon as well.

The first images over the screen showed a packed gymnasium, a makeshift school board podium, and a rumpled, angry board member, his placard on the table reading "Mr. Stevens," speaking passionately to the crowd.

"What is happening here must stop, and we, as a community must band together to stop it. How can we sit idly by while our students receive poor instruction, while their teachers quit teaching what they have been mandated by us to teach the children, especially at a point when so much is at stake for all of us just before the test? I believe that Mr. Willson, who started all of this by teaching a book instead of the test preparation curriculum, which is very expensive and which has been working for us so well for many years now, showed poor judgment. He has been swayed by one of our students, Sam Sanders, a reader of books no less and a truant from the March test. I question Mr. Willson's motives. What is his relationship with this boy, and with his mother? And how can we continue to support Dr. Dormont, who apparently supports their abberant behaviors, and has gone so far as to encourage the teachers to use books in class during these last weeks before the test, and proposing her own 'Project Huck Finn' for next year without consulting the board? This project would diminish the use of our curriculum and focus more on these so-called 'lost books.' I'll admit that I read *Huck Finn* way back in the 1970s, 50 years ago now – I didn't see the point of it then, and I don't see the point of it now. These people waste our time and money on a daily basis, defying the mandates of the school board. I will propose during our formal session tonight that they be dismissed, without benefits, their careers in education ended. And good riddance."

His remarks ended there, drowned out by cheering and jeering. He had more to say, but the board monitor had already warned him that his time was up. The crowd met his remarks in a bi-partisan manner, like a crowd at a championship basketball game during a heated moment when a referee's call goes, questionably, one way or the other. Half the crowd cheered wildly, standing and shouting, and the other half, just as vehement, jeered.

My spine tingled with excitement, expectation, and the thrill of the big story. I wondered out loud with the townsfolk packed into that room with me, "What in the world is going on here?"

23 – INTO THE NIGHT

In 26 years of covering local education news, I had never been to an event like this one. The board meeting lasted into the night; I finally looked down at my watch again at 10:00 pm, feeling a little like a cup of coffee would do some real good. But the meeting kept going, speaker after passionate speaker taking the microphone and making a point or two or a whole speech with regard to the issues at hand. I heard all sides. One side, Mr. Stevens' side, wanted the "nonsense" stopped, and for the board to exercise its formal authority to stamp out the rebellion. The other side, represented by Dr. Dormont and Mr. Willson, Sam Sanders and many of the other students, wanted the board to rethink its long-term commitments to the test and the test curriculum, and focus on other educational goals and possibilities.

Others spoke in conciliatory ways, hoping to find a common ground on which the parties could meet. Maybe there could be some way for the curriculum and the teaching approaches to change but for students to still score on the tests? This was new territory, however, with no one in the crowd possessing the experience or expertise in seeing that type of project through to results. The advocates of this position only saw the possibilities in theory. No one had pulled anything like this off before.

As with most events, the rhythms of the event changed. At some points, I saw the whole crowd and the board shaking their heads in agreement with the speaker. At some points, the crowd split, passionately jeering or cheering the speaker. Tensions and passions ran high.

Finally, the board president called for order at 11p.m. and made this statement:

"I am convinced of the passion and intellectual rigor behind all of the positions presented here tonight. But I'm tired, and the test is tomorrow. The children here have to get home and the rest of us, many of us, have other responsibilities associated with that event and our own lives. I move that we table our discussion until the next board meeting. In my mind there is no legitimate way that we can sort through all the issues and decisions without having more time to deliberate about what has been done and said," she paused for a moment, letting this sink in with the board and the crowd, "All those in favor say 'aye.' And the entire crowd said, 'aye.'"

But just as she prepared to lower her gavel and say, "Meeting adjourned," Sam Sanders stood up next to his mother and said, "Excuse me, Ma'am, but most of us will not be taking the test tomorrow." And with that simple sentence Sam walked out onto the gym floor and in front of the crowd. Many of the students sitting in the crowd up and followed him out. Their parents followed them. The crowd erupted again, this time in confusion and without order. The board president banged her gavel over and again, calling for order. The crowd would have none of it.

24 – THE DAWN OF DAY

I stayed at the school all night, interviewing everyone that I could. The last of the crowd left the building at around midnight. I took a short break to draft and phone in my story for the next day's paper by the 3:30 a.m. deadline, just under the wire. I had a wild ride overnight, part of which I spent exploring the book cave. It was amazing; I couldn't believe such a thing could exist in this day in age. I thought I had seen it all in public education. This day proved me wrong on that point. And I had a sneaking suspicion that I hadn't seen everything yet.

As the dawn brought a new day that got underway for the bus drivers as early as 6 a.m., I decided to stick close to Dr. Dormont, hoping to get the rest of the story on test day.

We began greeting buses and students together at 7:50 a.m. Dr. Dormont noticed how few students seemed to be getting off the buses and walking into school.

"I was afraid this would happen, but never in my wildest dreams did I think that the students and their parents would make the decision to boycott the test, and then actually do it," she told me, perhaps for the first time in a long time, at school at least, glowing with excitement.

In less than a half hour we had the statistics. Nearly 62% of the eighth grade class missed school. Mr. Jones stood by, waiting for his orders, but he and the deputy realized, along with Dr. Dormont, that the student body grossly overmatched them this time. They had a hard time using the word "truancy," something else had happened. The students and their families had decided to stay home and skip the test. They knew the ramifications, at least on first blush. Any school scoring under the state mandated minimum levels or who had no legitimate excuse for a low test-taker turnout would be taken over by state monitors and reconfigured, all of the administrators and teachers fired and rehired only after extensive re-interviewing. No second chances on this type of violation. The school would lose its guaranteed operating stipend and no other monies for faculty salaries or supplies would be coming into the district. Only a small operating budget would remain to support the transition to a new state-run administration and a small start-up staff of employees.

But this whole scene seemed to constitute a new situation, different from any that school people had ever faced in that area, or anywhere else in the state for that matter. No one knew what the state would do in a situation where the community members willingly boycotted the test and at least a significant portion of the school administration and teaching faculty supported the boycott as well. It had been 30 years since much controversy surrounded the tests at all. Most of the current rhetoric surrounding the tests had mostly to do with how students scored on them and how teachers prepared the students for the test, not with whether or not the tests were viable, legitimate measures of students' learning worth exclusive focus in an educational setting.

Dr. Dormont turned to Mr. Jones and asked him to continue working, "Please, Mr. Jones, start with Sam Sanders and work your way down the list. Let me know what you find out about these students – where they are and what they are doing. The information may prove to be important later."

"Yes, ma'am," he responded, and off he sped to track down the day's missing persons. He stopped by his desk and put the copy of *Romeo and Juliet* in his pocket.

25 – NIGHTFALL ON THE LAST DAY

The phone rang all day long. People took calls in the office, the staff doing its best to respond as adequately as it could with so little information. Of course, all kinds of calls came in, from reporters just hearing of the news, and from angry and disappointed parents. Some parents called in to report why they held their children out that day. Some lied, Dr. Dormont knew, saying their child came up ill that morning. Kids like Paul Johnson and Melissa McIntosh had never missed a day their whole school careers, and wouldn't miss unless a burst appendix or some other catastrophic act kept them out. Some parents said they kept their children home to protest the test.

The obligatory calls came in from the likes of Mr. Stevens himself, but Dr. Dormont wouldn't take his call, knowing that he was no ally and talking to him could serve little purpose at this point. Dr. Dormont did, however, take the three most important calls of the day herself.

The first call came from the school board president and superintendent early in the day. They had been such strong allies ever since Dormont had started as principal at Downing School. The school board president, Cindy's longtime friend, recommended that Dr. Dormont take the rest of the year off, including the faculty meeting scheduled for the following Monday and simply use up some of her personal days that had accumulated over the course of years. Dr. Dormont disagreed, and added, "Susan, if you are telling me I'm fired, then just tell me. But I'm just beginning to like this job again. I'd like to stay on."

The school board president agreed that she could stay, but she didn't know how she could protect her or her job in the coming days. "That's okay, Susan, I'll be all right. Goodbye."

The second call came from Mr. Jones around noon. He called from his cell phone reporting that most of the parents had their kids at home. He had stopped by Sam Sanders' house and found this note attached to the front screen door, addressed to him. He read it to her over the phone:

Dear Mr. Jones, We figured you would be here by 10 a.m. or so today, looking for us. Mom and I decided to visit her parents upstate. I won't be back til next school year. You can leave *Romeo and Juliet* in the mail slot next to the door, if you are finished with it. If not, you can let Ms. Belders at the library know that you have it. She'll like to know it's in good hands still. See you back at school. Sam Sanders.

"What's that *Romeo and Juliet* business about, Mr. Jones?"

"Oh, that's just something between me and Sam Sanders. Quite a kid, huh?"

"Quite a kid."

The third call came late in the day from the State Superintendent's Office of Testing and Instruction in the State Capitol Building. Ms. Hampton spoke to Dr. Dormont first. She tracked schools' scores all over the state on test day in order to clear up any technical problems schools had with the test. She asked Dr. Dormont a series of questions relating to the high absentee count.

"We have you down for a 62% absentee rate for the test today. How many of the students missed the test due to illness?"

Dr. Dormont replied, "Eight."

Ms. Hampton replied, rather concerned, "That's not evidence then that you have had some sort of catastrophic illness hit the school, is that correct?"

"That's correct, Ms. Hampton."

"How many students missed due to a natural disaster, a flood, for instance, bad storm, electrical failure, system failure, or some other physical defect in the building or the school system as a whole?"

"Zero, Ms. Hampton. Look, I know you have to ask all of these questions for the record, but I can tell you why the students didn't show up today. Would you like the answer?"

"Yes, Dr. Dormont, go right ahead."

"The students stayed home because they didn't want to take the test, and many of their parents and school people here agreed with them. We administered the test to the students who showed up. As you can see from the test scores already tabulated, they did very well."

"Yes, Dr. Dormont, they did well. But you didn't make the state minimum percentage of students taking the test, which you know is 97%. Also, while I haven't heard of such a thing in a long, long time, this situation calls into action our state intervention plan. You know what that means, don't you, Dr. Dormont?"

"I'm afraid I do, Ms. Hampton," Dr. Dormont replied.

I scribbled it all on my note pad, every detail. This was it, all coming down.

"I'll need to put you through to the State Superintendent, Dr. Norton. Please hold while I explain the situation to him…"

"She's putting me through to Dr. Norton, the State Superintendent."

"What does that mean?" I quizzed, knowing the answer.

"That means we're in big trouble."

After a few tense moments, the phone call continued.

"Dr. Dormont?"

"Yes, hello, Dr. Norton, how are you today?"

"I'm fine. You know test day is a big day here in the Capital. The question really is how you are doing?"

"Terrific, we've had quite a day here, too."

"That's what Ms. Hampton tells me. You do understand the ramifications of this situation, don't you, Dr. Dormont?"

"Yes, I do, sir, but these are extraordinary circumstances."

"Yes, well, at any rate, that will be up to me to determine. I'd like you to put the following procedures in place for shutting down your school until I can get there on Monday to discuss a state takeover with you, the superintendent, and the school board. First, dismiss everyone from the building and lock it down. Inform all personnel, especially the superintendent and school board president about our call. I'll be giving them a call as well. Cancel any weekend events that were scheduled at the school, whether school related or not. I'll be there at 10 a.m. on Monday morning to meet you. Is all that understood? I'll be sending a state police force of 10 officers to facilitate the shut down. They will be there in one hour to assist you."

"Yes, sir, except that Monday is our teacher work day and we had planned as a faculty to discuss all of the events of the past few weeks."

"Cancel it. I'll see you and the school board at 10 a.m. Monday. Goodbye, Dr. Dormont."

"Yes, sir. Goodbye."

Dr. Dormont stared blankly at the wall in front of her, stunned, but knowing that this moment had been inevitable from the beginning. She turned to me slowly and said, "The state is shutting us down in one hour. I need to get everyone out of here safely and word to everyone that the state will be taking over the school."

She began the process of dismissing the staff and writing the appropriate electronic memos to inform all affected parties. She wanted to have most of this accomplished within the hour, before the police arrived. In fact, she didn't want to be there when they came. She wanted to carry the memory of the day, their greatest day, with her, at least for the weekend. Dr. Dormont wanted things to end on her terms, not someone else's. Mission accomplished, she drove out of the lot, just behind me. I crept ahead of her, watching the incoming officers, their cars' flashing lights drawing attention to a vacated building. I drove home to write the story and to plan for my trip back on Monday to cover the official proceedings closing the school. Dr. Dormont drove home to read a good book, maybe one of the several hundred that lay in boxes in her back seat and trunk. Saved.

PART TWO:

SAM SANDERS RETURNS

27 – PICKING UP WHERE WE LEFT OFF

I met most of you during the first part of this story I wrote about Sam Sanders, *The Education of Sam Sanders*. As you recall, I typically write education columns for the *Record-Star* daily newspaper out of Fletcher. The *Record-Star* is one of state's last daily "papers" actually published on news print and delivered to homes and businesses – most news has been distributed electronically for a decade. Truth be told, I haven't seen anything like this story in the more than 20 years I've covered the city of Downing, where Sam Sanders lives and goes to school. You know from the first part of this story that Sam got most of his classmates and their parents to boycott the 8th grade test at the end of the school year. Of course, this didn't turn out so well for Dr. Dormont, the school principal, or the teachers at Downing, all of whom the State Department of Education fired on the spot that fateful afternoon.

Dr. Dormont's plan had been to spend the entire Monday following the test with the school's teachers figuring out how they were going to shift their curriculum and teaching approaches so that they could adequately address the growing interests of students and faculty members in going beyond the rote, mechanical, mind-numbingly boring computer-assisted curriculum they had been using for so long toward a curriculum that supported the engagement of students and teachers in more authentic learning experiences that actually had them reading, writing, and talking together about ideas.

Some teachers at Downing School like Pete Willson and Stephany Bellweather wanted to move quickly, immediately introducing the study of primary literature sources and class discussions and student writing projects. They even used real books that Harriet Hatcher had helped them secure from the age-old stash in the school's hidden basement room. Some teachers, however, like Teddy Hersh, vehemently resisted these notions altogether, seeing the idea of discarding an approach that works to keep test scores high as ill-informed if not downright idiotic considering all that is at stake with regard to the test scores: student scholarships, teacher bonuses, the school's budget, and ultimately, the school's existence as they knew it.

None of them thought the state would actually shut them down; few actually thought the students and their parents would stay home from the test. But Sam Sanders had touched a nerve, and history had been made. The State Superintendent for Instruction sent in the State Police to close the school and seize it. State Superintendent Norton merely followed the state guidelines for situations such as this; the fact of the matter is that most knew of the threat of school closure under such circumstances of a test boycott, but the power to do so had never been exercised before. Frankly, no conditions like this had ever existed under the longstanding laws surrounding school governance as set by the federal government and applied by individual states and local school districts. Some vaguely remembered the beginning of all this back in 2006 with the "One Size Fits All Act" created by a bi-partisan commission and signed into law by one-term President Penstock, but few recalled the details.

That law put the framework for standardizing curriculum through computer-assisted instruction across all grade levels in public education firmly into place, including the stipulations for dealing with districts that broke ranks and resisted change. No one understood how swiftly the state would take control because no state ever had to do it before. The state had supreme control, and it had never been challenged. Now citizens knew what would happen, in the late 2020s. The school would be shut down, quickly, and without ceremony.

Ultimately, the teachers never had a chance to meet that Monday or that entire summer, forbidden to do so by the state. Two glimmers of hope existed, though, for Dr. Dormont and her staff and community. The first was a lawsuit filed against the state by Ms. Susan Belders, the Downing Librarian, and Ms. Harriet Hatcher, the school media specialist. They contended that the state closed the school unfairly and illegally. The second was the return of Sam Sanders and his mother to Downing. Their absence during the summer months had been deeply felt by all involved.

The suit against the state, given how remarkable it was that someone was actually contesting a government decision, and how important it was for there to be a final disposition on the matter so that Downing citizens and their school could get back to business, made its way quickly through initial hearings. No one remembered the state ever being on the defensive like this. No one could remember there being so much at stake in such a short period of time in such a public venue. The lower courts quickly bumped the case up to the highest court, The State Supreme Court. No one could remember this ever happening, either. And no one could remember there being a kid like Sam Sanders, or so much energy being expended on education, schooling, children, and the issues that surround their upbringing and well-being. For decades schooling had been taken for granted, the decisions surrounding it having already been made and the procedures for delivering the curriculum well-established and rarely challenged.

No one could have ever dreamed up these events, or could have considered them a possibility, except in their wildest, most imaginative moments. So this is the nearly unbelievable story of Sam Sanders' return to Downing and his school. I never would have believed it if I hadn't seen it with my own eyes.

28 – A HOMECOMING

The August night felt still, even with the windows of Sam Sanders' and his mother's new Bramelder Motors Car rolled down all the way and the air lightly brushing Sam and his mother's faces and short hair. Absolutely nothing moved on the property like it usually did on homecomings, with animals rushing up and wagging their tales, waiting impatiently for their owners to emerge having been gone *so* long, usually only an hour or so. But it had been several months now since Sam and Betsy Sanders left town early in the morning on the day of the June test and basically vanished from view in Downing.

The time at Betsy's mother's house upstate served its purpose; it sheltered the family, especially Sam, from the media frenzy that attended the events surrounding the test boycott in June. Friends here in Downing said it was more than safe to come home now. Besides, school would be starting up again soon, they all hoped. Things would get back to normal.

Betsy Sanders had gotten a good job back in her old hometown upstate, inspecting baseball bats at the factory where her grandfather and father and brothers had worked so many years. And Betsy's mother put them up in cozy, cool beds and fed them and paid their bills back in Downing so collectors wouldn't come calling as soon as Bert Hoover started delivering the *Record-Star* early each morning again at their homestead in rural Downing. In fact, Betsy learned that her father had left her a sizeable sum of money after his untimely passing late last year. The money helped, but losing him had weighed heavily on them all, especially since Sam's Dad's passing had happened only two years prior. But like many families, talking about grief didn't do much good even if the talking miraculously occurred. Better just to live on, pouring the milk on the cereal for each other, and sharing parts of the morning paper with each other, and watching late night news on cinevision in silence with each other. That's what they needed, and that's what they gave, until it was time to move on. Betsy and her own mother knew how special and important this time would be for them to heal. Their time was up in August. They knew it, and packed their bags, and said goodbyes. They had come so far together, now it was time to venture onward, and apart again, by going home.

When the car's tires, and then their own feet hit the ground in the garage, they knew that much had changed on their old farm. Smooth, concrete floors had mysteriously replaced the old, soggy dirt floor. They could actually drive into the garage now and not sink into mud. And all the old rubbage had been removed and discarded and room for the car and for them to get out of it abounded. They had a good idea who had done the work, but they kept their silence about it, only a quick acknowledging glance let them know that each other knew who they each suspected had done the work as the garage door tilted and they drove onto the smooth new surface of their old garage: Pete Willson. The oil spot from Pete's old pick-up, the only scar on the new garage surface, had given him away. But they knew, even without this sign, that it must have been him.

Pete had been on the phone with Betsy and Sam periodically throughout the summer. He agreed to "watch" the farm: feed and care for the animals, take the dogs and cats to his house, and keep the place up as best he could until they returned. Betsy couldn't pay Pete, but there was no need to even speak about that. Betsy knew Pete's interest went beyond a few dollars for odd jobs. Sam had been listening in on the phone line during one of their last conversations, after they thought he had hung up and gone to bed:

"Betsy, It's just not the same around here without you and Sam. I never really knew it or felt it until you were gone, and I felt such a hole these past six weeks. I know it may seem fast to you, but I want you back in Downing, for good," declared Pete.

"My, my…one plate of chicken for a family meal and you're a suitor, Pete Willson? I thought it would take more than that…"

Their somewhat sickening laughter that followed drove Sam off the phone and onto the bed to ponder. He thought about that first chicken dinner that Pete had come for last spring, and about how he and his mother had made Pete a part of their lives so quickly. And just as quickly, lying on the bed, Sam decided this was a development he could stomach and not resist. Mr. Willson? Well, he was cool, and a good teacher, and he had a history with his Mom and family that meant something. And Mom, well, she was lonely, and so good. They deserved each other, and some measure of happiness after all that had happened.

And besides, he had his own mind on romance so he couldn't very well blame his Mom and Mr. Willson for theirs, at least what there was of it so far. Sam filled the entire long drive back to Downing with thoughts of Maggie Haley. Sam had known her so long, since first grade, but it wasn't until the walkout the night of the board meeting in June that he had felt her gentle touch on his arm on the way past the podium and out the door. He didn't even really become completely aware of her until they had exited the building and a crowd began to gather round them in the parking lot. Maggie had whispered to him with her hand still gently holding him by the arm, "You're a brave boy, Sam Sanders – I'm with you."

He couldn't respond to her with words, all flush in the face, speechless. He caught himself staring deeply into her green eyes, flabbergasted that he hadn't seen her care for him before, but thrilled beyond comprehension that she could say that to him, in the then and there, with the world swirling round them so. He touched her hand gently, too, and then squeezed it tightly, creating for him a lasting bond in that moment: she claiming him with a sentence, he claiming her with a look and a touch. She *knew* that he *knew* – and that he felt the same way; that's the important thing between two people at times like that. At least that's how Sam felt about it.

The boycott had created a new bond for them. Sam had begun calling her and writing to her over the summer. Maggie responded readily, and they had become a team, a pair, a steady couple, all over the phone line and through the mail. Sam couldn't wait to see her again, face-to-face. He had a feeling they would need and find comfort in each other in the coming weeks and months.

Once inside the back door, Sam caught his Mom's eye and they immediately raced for the phone. Betsy beat him to it, and dialed up Pete. While the phone rang, she consoled her son: "I won't be long. You want to talk to Pete?"

"I think I'll pass," Sam said, walking to the fridge to see if anything good to drink besides water, maybe a soda cannister or a juice cube, had lasted the summer in the fridge. He purposefully tried not to listen, though he couldn't have heard a word anyway since his Mom talked in a very hushed tone, like she wanted to hide something.

When she hung up, he came into the living room, "What was that all about? Why the hush-hush in your voice?"

"Nothing, Son, just Pete stirring things up a little. He says the lawyers for Ms. Belders and Ms. Hatcher want to see us at their offices tomorrow to talk about our testimony at the hearing."

"The hearing? I thought they were going to leave us out of it?"

"No, dear, apparently not. They need our help. I think we owe them that."

"Me, too, Mom, but I just want to go to school, you know?"

"I know, dear. It's only for a couple of days, and then they hope the court's ruling will secure at least an injunction so that Dr. Dormant can open up the school again."

"It's just that I always hoped high school would be fun, you know, not a big hassle. All of this trouble I've made out of things, well, it's taking me nowhere, do you know what I mean?"

"I do, Son, but I don't agree. This town has come a long way. Your school is way past where it was last year, just from what we've heard from other teachers and parents and students about the support you have and how they want the school to become a true place of learning again. Did you ever think we'd hear talk like that here in little old Downing?"

"Yeah, you're right, but I still wish I could get away from it. You know, it could die down a little bit. That would be nice."

"I know, honey, but that may not happen. Are you ready if it doesn't?

"Yes, ma'am, I am, I guess."

"Then it's off to bed now."

Sam turned to his Mother and kissed her goodnight. She had given up the "Goodnight, Sweet Prince" bit during the summer at Sam's request. He had grown out of it, he had told her, one of the latest ties to his childhood cut with little ceremony. It hurt her some to lose that part of their lives together, but new parts had sprung up, taking their place as he became more mature, a man, a high school freshman.

29 – SOME THINGS STAY THE SAME

Early the next morning, after breakfast and a trip round the yard to check out all of the improvements that Pete Willson had made to the property, including the new fence on the back lot where the cows grazed and the new loft in the barn for storing hay, Sam hopped on his bike and pedaled into Downing to see Ms. Belders at the library. He wanted to see her before the meeting with the lawyers, and he had asked Maggie to meet him there at 10 a.m. as well. He also had a slew of overdue books to return. After a summer of relative inactivity cooped up in his grandma's house, the pedaling winded Sam – the 20 books in the basket really weighed him down.

But the sight of Downing comforted him as he huffed and puffed along. Things looked the same, but so much different, too. Subtle things catch your eye when you return to someplace familiar after time away, especially from a small town. Like Mr. Stevens' house – it had painters hanging from all sorts of scaffoldings, painting the house a tremendously out-of-character crimson color. And the "First National Bank" sign had changed to "Second City Trust," and it had a cinevision-like screen sign out front with news updates scrolling across the bottom while pictures of Downing landmarks – city hall, the school, Stevens' factory – flashed on the screen. He hadn't seen anything like that put up "new" for years. Sam could hardly believe they made such things anymore – it must have come from some recycling warehouse, another attempt at making Downing look "historical," even retro, and perhaps more appealing to outside visitors.

When he reached the library, it offered true familiarity to Sam. The red brick building with majestic steps leading up to huge oaken doors looked exactly the same as when he left town in June. The town did nothing to keep the library up anymore anyway, mainly because there was no way it could look shabby. The exterior stood firm – large, smooth, red bricks bricks formed an aesthetically pleasing box shape with just a few ornate touches worked in here and there over the windows and doors. No shrubbery or lawn surrounded the building, so no weeds popped up through the concrete. The windows were tight and darkly tinted, hermetically sealing in the books and any other life that could thrive inside.

The library just *was*; it was going nowhere, it wasn't changing. The books inside remained the same. Only a small budget for buying new books – so few books existed anyway and they were outlandishly expensive – had been in place for decades. The only money left in a small endowment from the legendary Harvey Miles Foundation and left by a silent donor kept the library going, providing funds for the heating and cooling bills and for paying Ms. Belders a small salary. The library stood as a relic of the past, largely ignored by most citizens except Ms. Belders and Sam, and a few book-reading converts who had been paying attention to the controversy at the school and decided to join in by paying a visit or two to the library, revisiting childhood memories of favorite books, holding them in their hands and actually checking them out, taking them home, and reading them.

Since the library basically operated self-sufficiently and remained a rarity for a small town, the city kept it going and didn't encourage folks to build something else in its place. It was just fine the way it was, until now. The controversy at school had called into question the role of the library in public affairs. Stevens himself had been leading the charge to "reconsider" the role of the library in Downing's future. He wanted to annex the space for warehousing rare tools from his factory in a sort of industrial museum, really a tribute to himself and his business. On several occasions, Stevens had been seen harassing library-goers, even to the point of being told by the beat cops to cut it out or risk arrest.

As he entered the great building, Sam found Ms. Belders inside at her counter desk, as usual. She peered over her glasses at him as he entered, and without moving the book in her hand at all said, "Sam Sanders? Well, I'll be, I didn't expect to see you again so soon. You're not skipping out on the law again, or any such thing now, are you, Dear?"

As he approached her, she relented and put down the book and moved out from behind the huge mahogany countertop that separated her from library patrons. She hugged him full, like a long-lost child, and she squeezed him hard to her. She noticed immediately that Sam Sanders had grown about 3 inches since she had last seen him, and put on 20 pounds.

"My goodness, Sam, you are growing right out of your clothes. What is your mother feeding you?"

"Starch, mainly, you know, Ms. Belders, things kids like. Pizza and spaghetti mostly. Fried chicken. How are you holding up?"

"Well, that's another matter all together. Not so well, really. This lawsuit has me running every which way, I hardly have time for reading anymore. And I've been neglecting my duties here some. We've had over 40 patrons this month alone. You wouldn't believe it Sam. A mother read three whole books from Mary Denise Foster's 'Slippinsilious' series from 2003 to her three children one afternoon late last week and they sat at the table there and just laughed and laughed together. I haven't had so much fun, well, since you first came in and put me to work again."

"I'm glad to hear that you are busy, Ms. Belders. Sounds to me like you are doing your job better than you ever did it before. Your eyes were dancing there for a minute, you know, while you were telling me all that about the family reading the 'Slippinsilious' books," he replied.

She blushed, but quickly repelled him, "Well, full of flattery are you? Let's see what those books' overdue fees are going to run you before you get any more fancy with the words."

Sam smiled as Ms. Belders melted back into her character, and took the books out of his large knapsack. She pulled out the 20 volumes, mostly small fictional works. Sam had been working on novels from the mid 20th century most of the summer and enjoyed them immensely. As Ms. Belders calculated the fines, Sam wondered over to the stacks where books on education were kept. He explored the small collection of books on progressive education, what he understood to be a child-centered, experience-oriented approach to education that had some minor impact on teaching, curriculum, and schools in the 20th century. He saw names like John Dewey, and Deborah Meier, and Dennis Carlson, and pulled them down and skimmed over them, exactly what he was looking for.

When he approached her desk, Ms. Belders had gone back to her book, and looking over her glasses simply put up two fingers and said, "The fine is $2, Sam. How will you be paying today?"

He laughed, "$2? Come on, Ms. Belders, we know it's more than that."

"It will be more if you don't check out more of your favorites today," she jostled him.

"Yes, ma'am," he obeyed, pulling a $2 coin out of his pocket and plopping it on the counter with his new books.

"I see you are preparing for what lies ahead, Sam? Dewey, Meier, Carlson, classic progressives. I didn't know you knew anything about that."

"Well, I don't know much, but I take it now that you know something about it?"

She leaned down over the counter, put her face close to his, and whispered, uncharacteristically, "It's all I've been working on, Sam," she even grabbed his collar at the nape of his neck and pulled him close, intensely, "This case against the state has taken on a new life for me, it's absolutely inspired my reading about teaching and learning. I remember how much I loved most parts of school in my day, but I took for granted all that teachers did for me and my friends in the 1980s before this testing regime took over everything, way beyond materials and media for 'learning.' You come back when you finish those books, and let's talk some more."

She let go of him, gently smoothing his collar back, and lowering his small though growing frame back to the ground, and apologizing.

"Okay, Ms. Belders, I will," he said, marveling at her and what she had become to him, a trusted friend who would pull him close, even off the ground.

"I'll see you at the lawyer's office at noon, Sam. I have a few things left to do here. And it looks like you do, too," she said, nodding at the door, where Maggie Haley had just appeared.

30 – MAGGIE'S CHOICE

Sam's eyes met Maggie's from across the library hall, and they froze there for a moment. Ms. Belders saw it and laughed inside at their young love, recalling her own ancient experiences and indiscretions, and turned away from them to work on something else so that they could be alone. This might be the only place in the whole town where they could talk face-to-face, essentially alone. Maggie made the first move toward Sam and they met at the frame of light underneath the skylight in the entry alcove.

When they got close they grabbed hold of each others' hands stretched out in front of them. Maggie spoke first, and last.

"Sam, it is great to see you. I missed you so much... But I have to tell you something. My father decided to work for the state's side on your case. He's been waiting for a big break like this with his law firm out of Fletcher. Although he understands what you did and supported us at first, he needs me to step back from this so that I don't get in the way of his work. He can't very well have a daughter on the enemy's side of this. So I'm not going to be able to talk on the phone or meet like this anymore. I'm sorry."

Sam glazed over, his eyes misting, swallowing hard. The words stung, but little compared to the sting of Maggie's cold demeanor. Everything they had, which was everything to him, and apparently nothing to her, disappeared in just a few seconds, in a few carefully chosen words and sentences. She said it all so matter-of-factly, like a dentist calmly telling her patient she could make time on Friday or not to complete that root canal. Sam said nothing, merely nodding, holding firm while his knees shook and his ankles wobbled.

He took the hundredth, the thousandth, the millionth great disappointment of his young life in stride. Maggie simply walked out the door on him, bounded down the steps, and jumped on her bike and raced away. Numb, he just stood there and watched her go.

When Ms. Belders came out from behind the counter to make her way over to the law offices of Greene & Kilpatrick for their 10:30 a.m. appointment, she couldn't help but notice Sam frozen there under the blazing daylight of the alcove.

"What happened, dear? Where's Maggie? She was just here?"

"Gone, Ms. Belders. Gone..." Sam could barely squeak out the words.

"Well, she must have had an important appointment then, huh?"

"I suppose she did. Are you ready for the meeting?"

"Yes, sir. Will you walk with me?"

"Sure...Let's go."

Sam walked through the light, squinting to keep his sight and his balance, and walked out with Ms. Belders. One journey had ended it seemed, but perhaps another had just begun.

31 – A STRATEGIC PLAN

Sam and Ms. Belders walked into the usually quiet downtown offices of Greene & Kilpatrick and met a bustling crowd preparing for the morning briefing of their case, scheduled to be heard by the state's supreme court the next day in Richway, the state capital about 25 miles north of Downing. It's the first that Sam had seen of Dr. Dormont and Pete Willson and Harriet Hatcher in several months. When Sam and Ms. Belders entered the conference room they all three stood and extended their hands to Sam and Ms. Belders, exchanging handshakes, greetings, and kind words. They all looked relaxed and ready for what lay ahead. Sam's mom walked in and repeated the scene all around again with Max Greene and Mary Ann Kilpatrick on her heels.

Greene and Kilpatrick shook hands all around, too, after closing the door behind them. They quickly took charge of the meeting, and it's a good thing considering the preciousness of every minute with lawyers on the clock. Mary Ann led, welcoming them to the meeting and extending the courtesy of information about restroom locations in the building and the prevalence of fresh soft drink cannisters in the company cooler. Without a hitch, she went on to sketch Max's and her game plan for countering the state's application of the law to the Downing case:

"Now, keep in mind that we have little time during the hearing to make our case, and the Supreme Court members don't want us to bother with citing numerous, applicable cases in our oral arguments. That's all been done in our briefs. We have to hit home with serious, salient points with them. So...

"First..." she said, "we'll argue that the action to close Downing violated the community's right to due process in terms of arguing its position and unique circumstances to the State Superintendent for Instruction, Dr. Norton. By fiat, with little data, he seized the school when other options were available. Did Dr. Norton really have to send in the State Police? By law, maybe...but ethically, and given the lack of threat, was it necessary, practical, civil?

"Second...the teachers were not permitted to assemble peacefully and with due purpose after the close of the school day, even on their own time off school grounds. Citizens have the right to assemble, regardless of the topic, especially regarding things that reflect little threat to 'national security.'

"And Third...little has been said about the faculty's academic freedom. There must be leeway to interpret their role as educators to include the possibility of employing equally effective, culturally relevant instructional approaches – such as reading books or writing in journals – as opposed to merely carrying out the standardized curriculum. I had to dig a bit for that one, but I found some references to academic freedom in some old case law from the 1990s. I think it still applies, even though teachers have been doing something drastically different in schools of this century than they did in schools of the last century…

"Any questions?"

"Well, come to think of it," said Dr. Dormont, "I'm wondering what role any of us will play in the proceedings. Will you actually be able to call witnesses?"

Max jumped in, "Yes, Cindy, we plan to call you, and Pete, and Sam. We think we need to establish that the school was and still is in capable hands under your leadership. We need you to present a business-like, serious demeanor. We think we need to show that capable, veteran teachers were at the root of this movement, so we need Pete to appear scholarly, serious, able. And Sam, we need you to wow the judges with your intelligence, and child-like wisdom. So you need to remain calm, in control, sure of yourself, wise beyond your years."

"Max," Pete interjected, "with all due respect, your coaching makes this sound like a Wizard of Oz line-up – like you're hauling in the tin man, scarecrow, and lion with such and such qualities galore, and needing to show them for the court – but I don't think we can be all these things on purpose to the men and women in those robes and come off very well, very believable. I know how important it is for you and for us to plan, but I think we just have to tell our stories, and be sincere, be ourselves, and take it from there. Don't you, too, really? I get the gist of what you are saying and can live with that, but do you actually want us to rehearse this with you any further? If so, I can't see it. I think it will take away the passion, our focus."

Dormont, Belders, and Hatcher and the Sanders all nodded their approval at Pete. After all, what they had to say about what happened may not have all that much to do with the legal aspects of the case but everything to do with what might convince the judges, ironically, to hear them out and help them get their school back. The rule for this case held true: it isn't always about the law, but about what's right and wrong. And in this case they felt as though the Draconian Laws that have been applied so rigidly in the past make no room for the human spirit, for inquiry, for true, deep learning, for a great public education for every child. If they didn't claim this part of the debate at the moment of greatest import with the decision makers of society, then they would be forfeiting their chance completely.

"Well," paused Max, "…we know that you know we're the best. No one else could take your case and have a chance in hell to win it. Most people wouldn't even take it if they could argue it. But I'm putting pride and the law aside for now and telling you that I see your point. Just be ready tomorrow to do what you say you are going to be able to do. Because if you don't, the legal part of this doesn't hold up very well, and we may get blown right out of the room. Are you prepared for that scenario? I have to warn you about it, even given your hearty and defensible convictions."

Dr. Dormont spoke for the group: "We're ready Max. Don't worry about us. You just get yourself ready as best you can for us to have the stage we need and we'll deliver. We have the luxury of being right and being passionate about it. We know the other side feels the same way, but they don't share the grounds we are standing so firmly on. It's going to go well."

With that, the meeting broke up with more handshakes all around. The lawyers ventured off into their offices to make more formal preparations for the trip and for the hearing. The rest of them remained behind in the conference room, sharing a cup of coffee (pretty good for law firm stock), and catching up on their summers apart.

32 – SMOKING GUNS

They all entered the noontime street warily, shading their eyes from the glare of the hot Downing sunshine, digging in purses and pockets for sunglasses and moving toward the shelter of one of the last old maple trees on the town square. They all stood together, laughing and sharing summer stories. Once every one was quiet for a moment, Pete worried out loud for the whole group: "I don't think I have any smoking guns in my closet, sorry to mix metaphors on you..." they all laughed hysterically, mostly out of nerves, Pete wasn't *that* funny. He continued, "But seriously, this is very public, and when we get called to testify in the hearing, they could ask us anything, the lawyers or the justices. And our lawyers, as good as they are, haven't prepared us at all for that. I don't think I have anything to hide, but I know someone could twist things around and ruin one of us. I hope that doesn't happen, but I'm worried."

"Well, I have lived a boring, satisfying life with my cats and my books. I wish I had something to worry about, but I'll have to let you do the worrying on that front, Pete," said Ms. Belders, very matter-of-factly, and easing the tension.

"I suppose I'm in the same boat with you, Susan," said Harriet Hatcher. "My life in school and outside of school has been basically what it is on the surface, consisting of work, and very little play," her eyes brightened as she considered sharing a memory.

"One year, though, my Mom and I went to Vegas. Remember Vegas? We gambled and lost $1,000. We couldn't believe how stupid that was, but they were razing the old strip and putting in new government offices for the western territories. Remember that one-time only deal the government cut with citizens back in '09 not to audit gambling losses at or under $1,000? We took advantage of that. I still can't get over the images of Vegas going down in flames. What a year that was. What a loss that was, but it was worth it. I played about a hundred games of blackjack and lost my shirt. Those were the days..."

"All those great memories and you lost your money. Just think what it would have been like had you won, Harriet," chimed Betsy. They all laughed heartily again.

"Which brings us to *us*," Betsy gripped Sam's shoulder tight to hers and kissed his cheek. "Lord knows I've had my wayward times. But meeting your Daddy was the best thing that ever happened to me. You're here because of that, and we have a life now because of him. Don't you worry, Sam, if they dredge up the things your Dad got himself into with Stevens. He was right to work for workers' rights, and Stevens had no business coming down so harshly on him. The question is, do you have anything to hide?"

The question rather surprised the rest of their friends, after all Sam was only 14, and going into only the 9th grade. He couldn't drive yet, and as far as they knew hadn't been running with rowdy friends. They did know about Maggie Haley, though, and they knew of her father's work on the other side of the case, the state's side.

Sam shrugged his mother's arms off his shoulders, politely but decidedly and addressed the group: "I guess you all know that Maggie's father is working for the state against us, and you should all know that Maggie cut me loose today because of it. I didn't argue with her, I knew there was no way to keep on going with her given the magnitude of the situation. But I told her some things that I'm worried she might say back to the judges. I told her some of the books I'd read, including some of the titles that have been on the banned list that even Ms. Belders couldn't get for me. I told her about Marx, and Friere, and Pikestone. She hadn't even heard of them and we talked on the phone about them… I don't know, it's probably nothing, but I realize I shouldn't have ever said anything about them, but I just had to get the ideas out… I'm so sorry…" his head drooped to his chest in shame.

Everyone in the group reached out for him, and patted him on the shoulders and consoled him. It's a good thing they did because right then, as he looked up at his well-wishers, Sam saw a man crouching on top of the city building with a gun. He could hardly believe it, and barely eked out a warning while he pointed upwards, "Look, it's Stevens with a gun! Duck!" So everyone scrambled to the ground, in fearful disbelief. Then they immediately heard the sound of a lone shot and the resulting contact the bullet made with the great limb of the maple tree they were standing under.

33 – THE CHASE

They all hit the ground, and they stayed low, scampering behind nearby trashcans and cars and park benches to avoid another shot. Sam peaked from behind the maple tree's trunk and noticed that the parking cop, Officer Burt Harold, who had been passing by giving out tickets just moments before, of course had heard the shot and had heard Sam yell out the name "Stevens" and had seen him point in the direction of the shooter. Harold got up quickly and began running toward the building where the shot came from. Sam, instinctively, because he boiled more with anger than with fear, ran after him, and after Stevens.

Pete tried to trip Sam by the leg, reaching out to grab him, to keep him from running toward danger, but Sam avoided him, skillfully jumping Pete's arm. His legs pumped wildly, his arms, too, and he caught up with Officer Harold after about 50 yards. Harold looked to be in decent shape, still basically walking a beat everyday as a parking cop, but Sam was young, and strong. They both reached the side of the Burke Restaurant Building at the same time. Harold put his arm over Sam's chest, holding him back.

"Son, this is as far as you go," Harold said to Sam, not looking at him, but instead concentrating on getting his revolver out of its holster. It had never been drawn before, except in drills with other cops.

"I'm going with you. I want Stevens. He took a shot at me, for heaven's sakes."

Harold peered around the corner, and there was Stevens running away down the alley away from them. He saw Stevens toss the old rifle in a trash bin, just like in one of those old crime dramas he had seen on cinemavision years ago. He'd actually seen repeats of old television shows from the 1990s on "cinemavision extra," way late at night on one of his many sleepless nights. He couldn't believe Stevens was actually stupid enough to ditch the weapon in a place so likely to be searched. He stepped into the alley and yelled and pointed his revolver, "Stevens, halt, police…!"

But Stevens kept running. The old man was getting away, hell bent on running.

Harold began the chase down the alley, now that Stevens had disarmed himself, as far as he knew. He felt confident that he could apprehend him without incident now. He didn't think about Sam anymore, because Sam, who could have easily passed Officer Harold running down the alley, adjusted his strides to stay one step behind Harold all the way.

Stevens took a few lame turns to try and lose them, cutting through a few yards and around an old shed or two, but he never made it out of their sight, and they began gaining steadily on the old man as he tired. They had gone about a half a mile when the gap closed to just a few yards. Stevens attempted to hop a three foot steel fence and caught his pant leg on the top of one of the posts, and fell awkwardly over the fence, his pant leg still stuck to the post and the rest of his body dangling over, writhing in pain as he attempted to get free from the impossible obstacle.

Officer Harold jumped the fence, with Sam right behind, and he lifted Stevens roughly off the fence, slamming his face and chest back against the fence and violently pulling both of his hands back behind him and cuffing him. Harold was a little out of breath, but he had it on the ball enough to tell Stevens to keep quiet, that anything he said or did could be used against him in a court of law. Stevens' rights. Stevens said he understood, and as Harold wheeled Stevens around, they both confronted Sam Sanders, Sam's fists both clenched and his brow furrowed into a violent, nasty grimace.

"Stevens, you coward! Why did you shoot at us? What's your problem?"

Officer Harold let Stevens talk. He wanted to know the answer, too, though he knew it wouldn't help Stevens, only hurt him. He put aside the moral dilemma for a moment.

Stevens screamed, "You're the problem, Sanders, you and your Dad and every-one like you...!" Now Stevens seethed, shaking from fatigue and pain and hatred. "People like you think you're better than everyone else," he foamed now at the mouth, sickened by the very idea of Sanders, let alone the physical reality of him standing there. "Reading books, and making trouble, and getting folks stirred up with a little bit of education? That's your game. *Huck Finn*? That's not what they want, they want to live and get by. But no, you have to go around saying there's something better, another idea, or something else new under the sun. I don't even know you, but I hate you and people like you. You jeopardize everything that is good and decent about this society. You're disobedient and impolite, and just flat out wrong. We should hunt all of you down, and take every one of you to task, eliminate you until we have what we need, people who will listen and do what they're told. You make me sick, and I'll get you even though I didn't get you today. I'll spend the rest of my life trying."

"Okay, you're done, old man," Harold said to Stevens, himself sickened by his stupidity and hatred. He dragged him through the alley past Sam and back toward town.

Sam just stood there, in disbelief, and stared at the strange scene taking its final shape: A hateful old man with a broken ankle being drug off by a cop – who never in 18 years on the force had apprehended a criminal or had even *seen* a criminal act taking place – after taking him on a chase through town after trying to kill a mere kid for no good reason with a bad shot out of an old, clunky rifle that he discarded into a trash bin in plain sight on the run like an idiot criminal out of some 1990s TV show.

How could it have come to this? What could possibly happen next?

34 – THE SHOW MUST GO ON

That night the town buzzed. Phone trees started up, with people calling each other to find out more about what had happened on the street, to get the scoop, and then calling other friends to fill them in. Cinemavision sent a reporter out to Downing and townspeople watched the report of the day's events on the 8 p.m. news. Most couldn't believe it. Commentators asked, "Why would a wealthy old man with a successful business throw it all away by taking a potshot at a kid?" It just didn't make sense to anyone. The town hadn't seen a public display of hatred or lunacy like this in a long, long time.

Mostly well-wishers called the Sanders residence, but Betsy took the phone off the hook after about 30 calls because some of the last callers had been angry. She didn't tell Sam about these, the ones that started, "Shut that kid up or I will finish Stevens' work!" The calls were constant, and mostly heartening, but Sam and Betsy needed space to deal with the day's events. They were exhausted from the hours spent at the police station giving statements and then just coming down from the adrenaline rush. They had been shot at, and that didn't happen every day. Not in these parts, and usually not in a lifetime.

After supper, Sam and Betsy sat in silence watching the news. They wondered off to bed about 10 p.m., and without really thinking about it, Betsy came into Sam's room and sat down on his bed. She hadn't done that in years, since she read her last bedtime story to him back in elementary school. She took his hand in hers and just held it for a time, and brushed the hair on his forehead over to the side, lovingly. Finally, she asked, "Sam, are you okay?"

He turned his head away from her; he didn't want her to see his tears. He looked out the window until he could catch his breath. She continued to hold his hand, so gently. Waiting.

"Mom?" he said, still looking away, "I lost Maggie today and that jerk Stevens shot at me. Gee whiz…that's a lot right there. And tomorrow we have to go to Richway and testify before the Supreme Court? My, it's just so much…I want to know why Stevens hates me so much that he wants me dead. Why don't people want to open the school back up, with Dr. Dormont and others there? How did the test take over to the point that we don't value ideas, and books, and thinking? How could this happen? And why doesn't anyone see it? There's hardly any public debate about any of this. There's no public dissent at all. None that I can see or hear. We just accept what has been handed to us by the powers that be, what we hear on cinemavision and read in the paper, and citizens don't act much like they have any recourse. They just follow around blindly, day-by-day, just doing their small part to keep the machine running? But does the machine do anything remotely oriented toward benefiting us?"

Sam stopped there, and turned to her finally, "Mom, what am I going to do with all of these questions in my head? It isn't right for a 14 year old to have them, is it? How did I get them in my head, and why can't I get them out?"

Betsy stayed quiet for a few moments, collecting herself, thinking of Paul, stroking Sam's hair, looking deeply and firmly into his eyes, at a life ablaze with life and vigor, so much promise.

"Honey, I don't know. I honestly don't. But I'll tell you what your father used to say. He used to say, 'People are just scared, Betsy, that's all. They don't think for themselves anymore because all of their rights have been taken away and they got a little soft with cinemavision and they have all they think they need. We have to get their rights back, and their ability to use them to get access to knowledge and power. All we see is what others want us to see. That has to end or people will live in chains, not free.' That's why he led the literacy brigade at the plant and that's why Stevens hated him and us so much. Stevens could control his workers, even the smart ones, because they never learned anything about organizing labor or working toward fair working conditions or wages. They never learned about labor in school, they never saw programs about it on cinemavision and they didn't have access to books about it. That's why your father – no matter how good he was, and innocent – posed a threat to Stevens. You posed a threat, too. That's why Stevens shot. He can't control you and he knows it."

"So what's to keep other crazy people from shooting at us?"

"Nothing, Son, it could happen again. The question is, 'Will we let fear stop us?' I come from a fearless stock, you know, and so did your father. And courageous people like Cindy and Harriet and Susan surround you, Sam. They would take a bullet for you. We've come this far, and tomorrow we finish it. Okay?"

"But it may not be that simple, Mom. We don't know what the judges will say, or what the lawyers will do, or how the public will react."

"No, we don't. All we have is faith that right will win out, that we will be fairly heard, and that some little bit of commonsense and insight will reign. I trust that it will. This little bit of trust and faith are really all we have, and each other, which counts for a lot. It's enough to stake everything on. We'll be fine." She smiled and hugged him close, pulling him up from the bed. His arms around her, Sam felt safe. He felt her will, strong, and unshakable. He closed his eyes and slept for tomorrow.

35 – THE STATE

The next day, friends gathered at the Sanders' house with their cars and formed a caravan for the family, falling in front of and behind the Sanders' car with theirs so as to protect it, at least symbolically, from anything that might attempt to derail them on their way. After all, it isn't everyday that innocent people get shot at in Downing. No one knew what might come next. All the cars and passengers made it to Richway safely, without incident, pulling up to the Supreme Court steps and letting the principal parties out so they could enter the building quickly and without ceremony. But reporters and cameras ringed the entire building. The Downingites realized they would have to run the gauntlet just to make it inside.

All of the cars, about 20 in all, opened their doors and let people out at about the same time. This was all unplanned, but it worked out so that the reporters didn't know whom to talk to. They scrambled from car to car asking, "Are you the Sanders family?" Luckily, Sam and Betsy squeezed unnoticed by a set of reporters. By the time they had been identified, the reporters could only chase them up the steps. The reporters didn't catch them in time to question them, because the state police intervened and basically took the Sanders into protective custody and inside the building. Inside, a mob with questions loomed and they shouted with their microphones extended for comment, "How does it feel to be shot at? Why are you pressing this issue in your school? What about your relationship with Pete Willson?" The Sanders made no comment, and were simply happy to make it to a holding room before entering the court for the hearing.

When it was time, the state police led them to the Supreme Court Chambers. They had just sat down, when the Chief Aide to the Court entered ahead of the Justices and shouted, "All rise!" The crowd did so, and remained standing until all of the judges sat, folding their long, black robes under them so they could sit comfortably, and then the assembly sat down all together. Then the Aide read from a scroll, "Hear ye, all citizens here gathered, the Supreme Court of this great state will sit for the case of 'Belders, Hatcher, & Dormont v. The State.' All rules and rights of this great court now take precedence over any other civil authority. Quiet please…"

The Aide yielded to the Chief Justice, who adjusted her glasses and then banged the gavel hard, with such authority that she seemed almost angry.

She said: "I want you to know that all of the court's justices are aware of the events of the past 24 hours in Downing. We want to express our condolences and best wishes to all of the people who have been affected by the events of the past few hours, and really, of the last few months. All of the justices have read the briefs, and would like to hear from two witnesses, whom *I* will question. The lawyers assembled here can advise their clients, but please do not interrupt the proceedings with questions of your own or other stray comments that might distract from our work here today. Gallery members are to be quiet; any noise from you will cause your immediate removal by the Aides without question. The bottom line is to determine how to deal with the breaches made by the school district in terms of the long-term viability of the school, and perhaps, of our public education system as it exists today."

"In the questioning process, I am invoking the 'Chief Justice Act of 2015' which states that 'a Chief Justice may suspend the usual questioning procedures in a hearing – typically involving all of the justices assembled – and engage as sole questioner a limited number of witnesses in order to expedite the hearing and the deliberation process for the court.' It's kind of like getting a good hand in a euchre game and playing the hand alone without your partner. I hope this moves us quickly through the process and that we can give a decision today. Personally, I've never been a firm supporter of the Act, nor have I ever invoked it, but today I think it serves our purposes well. We'll get to the bottom of things quickly."

"For your information then, first, we would like to hear from Maggie Haley. The transcript of her deposition impressed us. We want to know some more about what she thinks of the matter…Maggie Haley? Please rise and take the stand in front with the Court Aides' assistance…"

The courtroom fluttered with anticipation and suspense. Both sides had worked so hard at preparing witness lists and practicing testimony that the judge's mandate caught them off guard. But the lawyers for the state adjusted quickly, taking a few brief moments to coach their star witness. Everyone knew now that Maggie would be the first one examined; no one knew who the second would be, and the lawyers were too frightened of the court, at this point, to ask.

As Maggie made her way up to the stand, she glanced at Sam and smiled. He smiled back; ultimately, Sam couldn't resist her.

Maggie trembled a little as she placed her small hand on the huge stone tablet and repeated, "I swear to tell the truth." After she sat down, the Chief Justice gave the people in the room a chance to settle down. The Chief Justice merely held the gavel and stared blankly, sternly out over the crowd, demanding, without words, silence.

36 – PRELUDE

The Chief Justice began the questioning with a very simple request for Maggie: "Maggie, please tell the court what you know about Sam Sanders."

Esquire Greenfield, sitting right next to Sam, couldn't stand being silenced or the nature of the question. So he leapt to his feet and pleaded with the Chief Justice:

"Please, Chief Justice, is it appropriate to turn these proceedings into an attempt to assassinate the character of my client, a 14 year old boy, who just wants to read books in school?"

"Mr. Greenfield, I take it?" the Chief Justice asked rhetorically, and very calmly as she glanced down at the lawyers' roll call and easily determined Greenfield's identity as lead counsel. "I'm going to let you stay in this court for the rest of these proceedings. But I won't tolerate another outburst on your part or anyone else's. I'll have you removed by the Aide if you say another word here. This goes for anyone else on staff or in the gallery," she peered over her glasses, accusing the crowd, before continuing. "Also, I'm giving you no justification for questions I ask in this court. This is the line I'm taking. Please sit down, and be quiet."

Greenfield sat down, sheepishly, but knowing that his outburst was necessary for limiting whatever pressure on Sam that would come to bear from Maggie's testimony, no matter the ignominy it might bring to him personally.

Meanwhile, Maggie squirmed in her chair, looking up first at the ominous array of justices in their long black robes behind a huge oaken counter, and then looking down second at her family and friends and community members assembled in the courtroom, and then last at Sam.

She smiled briefly. Then she spoke quickly, and with confidence into the microphone, remembering the Chief Justice's question without being prompted again.

"I've known Sam Sanders as a friend in school for about five years, since we moved to Downing from Richway and I started school there. We've been classmates all that time, and in the past year or so we've become better friends. I don't think Sam ever noticed me much from across the classroom or in the lunchroom until after the big school board meeting where he walked out – actually, I'm sorry – where *we* walked out, saying symbolically that we weren't going to take the test. I wound up taking the test, however, even though I basically supported Sam and what he said about school, in general. But my parents thought it was irresponsible for me to miss that day and hurt the school, so I showed up on test day and took the test."

"I did enjoy Mr. Willson's class while we read *Huck Finn*. I've never had a school experience like that, and that's probably where I started noticing that I liked Sam a lot. He is so smart, and he has read so much. Sam contributed so much to the discussions; I learned as much from him and my other classmates about the book and what they thought. Many of my classmates, myself included, had never read any book all the way through until that class. And as things heated up around the school in terms of how people were talking about our class, I got more in tune with Sam and what he was saying and doing."

The assembled masses listened to her every word, enthralled with this girl of 14, so eloquent, so self-assured. So few people had ever heard a young person talk like this; she had them mesmerized, including the justices. She continued.

"Then this past summer we became something more to each other. There was nothing physical about it, except for a touch on the hand that we shared after the events of the school board meeting in June. Sam went off with his Mom after that to get some space away from the controversy flying around. And we started talking on the phone. I called him first, and he was so sweet. We probably talked on the phone every night this past summer. Some nights I got really interested in what he was saying and what he was reading, but it concerned me, too. I didn't really understand everything he was talking about and I hadn't read the books he had read so I really didn't know what to think about it all." Here Maggie began to falter, looking down at her folded hands in her lap, and going mum. Maggie stared down blankly, as though in a stupor, completely silent.

The Chief Justice intervened; the silence deafened even her. "Maggie, what was it about these conversations that upset you, or concerned you the most?"

Maggie composed herself the best she could, and looked straight into Sam's eyes: "I just felt he had become so *radical*. He had been reading works by Paolo Friere, the long forgotten Brazilian pedagogue who taught peasants to read and ultimately to question the undemocratic processes that kept them in subservient roles in society, in politics, in the economy. Sam said that we were even worse off than these peasants, rich in things but clueless about all that society had stolen from us by making it nearly impossible for citizens to access any information or knowledge that would free us from the bondages of race and class and gender, and of control by the dominant arm of society, the state, and its chief aide-de-camp, the public school. He said that even though we lived under the umbrella of a representative democracy, only people with privilege and great wealth had any real access to power, that is the ability to make any substantive changes in the life conditions of all citizens, especially those who have the least."

Then she took a deep breath and went on, with great courage, a small tear welling in the corner of each eye, not so much for Sam but for the pressure: "He began to tell me about Lenin, and how he helped overthrow the czar and led the Russian revolution early in the 20th century, and about how Stalin became the first dictator of the Soviet Republics, long defunct now but held up as ideal by Sam when he talked. Sam talked about how perfect Lenin's vision was for a Marxist society and a communist government that would provide everything that all needed without reservation and with the ultimate commitment, each according to his or her need. I asked him if he really thought these ideas were applicable to us, if he thought we could be communists, or socialists. For heaven's sakes, I don't even know if there are any socialists left in the world, except for the Swedes, and we all know what happened to them…"

The entire courtroom giggled in recognition of Maggies' great wit, despite her internal torture, the whole company remembering the rich fix the Swedes had gotten into when they tried to save communist Cuba with a monetary bailout in 2010, and wound up begging the world for relief once the regime fell, the crooked leaders of the falling regime having stolen all of the trillions that had been invested by the generous country and depositing it all in inaccessible bank accounts all over the world. Sweden remained steadfast, undaunted by it all, though it was frequently mocked by the rest of the west as the last socialist democracy remaining on the earth.

"Please continue, Maggie, and you should know that we can do without your editorializing."

"I'm sorry, Ma'am, I didn't mean to be disrespectful. Anyway, once I knew what was going on in Sam's head, and what was going on with the case by the state against him, I realized that I needed to cut whatever ties we had. I did that just yesterday, at the library, my first chance to do it since he returned from upstate. I regret that I had to do it, but it was for all of our own good. I hope we can still be friends. I know how hard that is, though, in situations like this. Who knows what will happen next?"

From broken to steely, Maggie had shown the range of her colors and had done damage to Sam that may have been beyond repair. Even as her own ego flourished on the stand, she knew she had done harm. Maggie had been fazed, but remained unchecked. She was innocent, though simultaneously and completely absorbed by the power of the status quo.

Maggie fell silent again and looked down again at her hands. Sam's head had dropped as well. He couldn't bear to look at her. The Chief Justice dismissed Maggie while the courtroom buzzed. No one could believe that the Chief Justice hadn't pressed her further. Without ceremony, the Chief Justice called her next witness, "That's enough Miss Haley. Would Sam Sanders please rise, and take the stand?"

38 – RESISTANCE

Sam took the stand with a grace similar to that of Maggie. He walked quietly, humbly up the steps and sat softly in the chair, his hands folded on his lap and his eyes looking straight up at the Chief Justice.

She lowered her eyes onto him, and then onto the Aide, who had to pull Sam's attention away from the Chief Justice and then onto the obligatory stone tablet, upon whose surface Sam laid his hands and repeated the familiar ritual retort to "tell the whole truth."

The Chief Justice began, "Sam Sanders, you've heard the brief but pointed testimony of Maggie Haley. We know what happened at the school last June, before and after the test, from numerous written briefs and from our own knowledge of the setting and events there. We have an idea from Maggie's testimony about what you were saying to her and thinking about these last months. But we need to hear from you so we can make a preliminary decision about what to do with you and with your school. Clearly, your school violated the law. What we are wondering, which is new ground for us, is whether or not your reasons for resisting were rational and in any way justified or not. Do you understand?"

"Yes, I do," he replied.

"Then tell us, how is it that you came to be a reader of books?"

"Well," said Sam, "my father read books constantly, even after they began going out of use because of the switch to computer-based texts in school and in almost every other walk of life in which reading was important. He just loved books, we talked about them all of the time. We read books together sometimes, and we'd talk about them over dinner. These are some of my best memories of my Dad, whom we lost two years ago in a car wreck. He was a good Dad, and I suppose I'm a reader of books because of him. My Mom and I just kept right on reading together, it didn't stop. She encouraged me to visit the library and our friend Ms. Belders there. Ms. Belders helped me find all of the titles I wanted, and even went out of her way to get books from other libraries, even though that was difficult to do sometimes. We became friends."

Ms. Belders smiled at him from her seat in the gallery, proud to have been part of his upbringing, a friend for life. But the Chief Justice intervened. She wouldn't allow Sam to gloss over his relationship with his father and the potential implications it had for the current situation.

"Sam, tell us some more about your father, what happened to him, and your relationship," the Chief Justice queried.

Sam continued.

"Obviously, all of this was bound to end up badly somehow. Dad started reading all of the time, sometimes skipping work at Stevens' plant to read a book he was excited about. He had been pleading with Stevens to create a reading lounge with magazines and books in it for the workers to use on break times. But Stevens thought Dad had ulterior motives, being an activist and all for workers' rights. This led Stevens to get rid of Dad, even though he was a valuable worker and respected by the rest of the employees. It caused quite a stir, not because there was anything that Dad could do about getting fired, but because of the fact that anyone cared at all about someone else getting the ax. I think it drove Stevens crazy, people asking him all the time when Dad was coming back to work, and wondering why he fired him for something so seemingly harmless, and Stevens not bending at all. But neither Dad nor I kept reading in order to put Stevens out of business or to overthrow the government or to close down the school. We just wanted to read, and believe we had a right to do it."

Here Sam paused, and carefully weighed his next thoughts.

"I read some 20th century pieces that had to do with citizen action, including civil disobedience, against the government. While a certain thread of conservative patriotism has always run through our middle class American society, especially during and after times of great fear from terrorist attacks or wars, people still had the right to resist the government and its representatives and even its laws on moral grounds. And they did so. Sometimes they were imprisoned, but mostly they found haven in institutions such as courts and found a way to make their case. Everyone understood how important this type of freedom was for society and how important it was for different institutions to check each other when they got out of balance. How else would we have made progress on civil rights, on labor rights, on gender rights?"

"In recognition of all the ground we've lost in the last decades, Dad wanted to reinstitute one of the old traditions of the labor movement, educating workers to fight for human and workplace rights in their own settings. When he made so little progress at Stevens' plant and got fired, he stayed home all the time, and started drinking. He shouldn't have been driving that night he died. I can't explain anything more about that." Sam collected himself; he decided not to cry this time.

"What may have set Stevens off, to the point that he would take a shot at me, is the realization that I'm not going away. I might be kicked out of school, and lose my job someday, and even start drinking, but I'm going to keep reading and speaking up. I'm just made that way. What surprised me and pleased me the most last year was how my teachers and Dr. Dormont responded to me. At first, my actions seemed to hurt and threaten them. But then they really came around. Ms. Hatcher, the school librarian, read *Catcher in the Rye* with me. Dr. Dormont, our school principal, let Mr. Willson teach *Huck Finn* to my class. School started going so well I began to enjoy going. Everyone knew I wouldn't take the test. Something has to give, Judge, you know? How much longer can we continue going to school and spending all day reading these boring, short texts and answering inane questions, completely de-contextualized from who we are as citizens and as a community? Then society bases its decisions about people's lives on these tests we take, and they really don't tell us much of anything about the person, just that he or she can bubble in the right letter after memorizing the right 'facts.' There is so much more to learn than what we learn for these tests. Some questions I would have are, 'What do you read to get to be a judge? What do you read to make yourself a better judge? It can't just be the non-fiction pap they feed you through the computer, can it? Or merely piles and piles of books on case law?'"

Sam looked up at her, politely, humbly, genuinely expecting an answer.

The Chief Justice laughed to herself, nodding all around the courtroom in recognition of something she had lost long ago, or at least hadn't seen in quite a while. In deference to him, she turned to Sam to address him.

"Sam, schools today aren't made for you. We made decisions decades ago that we didn't need any more people like you, in general. We decided that the costs of an education like the one you want didn't match the typical payback we got from most children. Sometimes smart kids like you didn't do well on the test, like your father, I've heard, and so some policy makers and decision makers began questioning the point of public education. And in their eyes, most children just didn't show any interest in ideas, or maybe teachers just got tired of the deeper project of teaching, and how hard it is to teach things like caring, freedom, liberty, love, beauty, thoughtful criticism, reasoned resistance to authority, and on and on. We took a much easier route, one that's cheaper and less strenuous to follow, and I'm afraid we've lost quite a bit. I am forever amazed at how bright and able young people like you and Maggie turn out despite what we do to you in schools, and in courtrooms. I want to give your parents credit for that."

She paused for just a moment, pondering her next thought, but Sam rebutted before she could speak."

"Thanks, Judge, but what do you read?"

The entire courthouse laughed politely at Sam's naiveté, knowing in that instant that he would be forgiven by the Chief Justice, and perhaps that she would give an answer.

After a pregnant pause, and an accusing look at the gallery not to push it too far past this near point-of-no-return, she responded, "Well, in answer to your question, Sam Sanders, I've read piles of case law, and that's important, but more important for me is that I continue to read constantly from my own personal library, the one I collected at college before most college courses went online. It's in the basement of my home, no doubt a lot like the one Dr. Dormont and her friends built in your school. I go there quite often, alone, and read, and think. That time has had a huge impact on my career, and who I am today as a person."

The Chief Justice paused briefly after this confession, then took quick action, addressing Sam, and then the whole courtroom:

"Well, so much for our little conversation. I want you to step down please, and return to your seat. We'll adjourn for an hour and we'll render a preliminary decision. That decision will bind all parties until a more formal set of proceedings is brought forward, if at all."

The Chief Justice banged her gavel and said, "This courtroom is adjourned until 11 a.m."

The shocked gallery buzzed. Sam stepped down to his waiting family members. Maggie Haley quickly exited the courtroom with her mother and father in tow.

39 – THE DOWNING CROWD, E PLURIBUS UNUM

The crowd milled around the lobby areas of the courthouse, eating snacks and talking while all waited for the justices to return. Pockets of conversations erupted, most of them joyful, not somber. One large group of citizens focused on the proceedings of the morning, commenting in stiff murmurs about the Chief Justice's approach to the morning session and her invocation of the 2015 Act giving her sole reign in the courtroom. Many of the folks from Downing hadn't seen each other for much of the summer as a result of summer vacations and school being out, so long lost friends and even relatives greeted each other with joy and spent time catching up on local and family news. Others just milled about engaging in small talk, killing time. As a rule, the "everyperson" citizen of Downing viewed the events of the day as typically working out in his or her favor, usually. Things going wrong and staying wrong wasn't how their lives usually worked. So they expected the justices' decision to be favorable.

And anyway, deep down, what was the point of fretting? Even if things didn't go their way, and the school was not allowed to reopen with its former staff at the helm, they still had to figure out a way to do school. Not all of them were sold on the ideas that Dr. Dormont, and Pete Willson, and Sam espoused. But they remained aware of the possibilities, and saw the merits in their positions, and valued their steadfastness in taking a position and then action despite the risks. No matter what, the bottom line remained – some sort of school would be starting in a few weeks. They just wanted to know what kind of school it would be.

The reporters on site in the lobby mostly crowded around Sam and his family, though there were fewer in number of them than there were of those others clamoring outside at the doors and windows for even a glimpse or a word from Sam. Sam and his Mom talked politely to the reporters, consistently answering the same questions the same way over and over again, the best they could. They had a hard time understanding the fuss, but like any human being would, they relished the limelight a bit, basking in it to some degree, though deeply longing for the most part to be left alone. They lived in this funny tension, simultaneously seeking out the light, while knowing it might burn them at any moment.

What Sam didn't expect to happen amidst the continuing hubbub was to see Maggie Haley. She appeared around the corner without her parents, near the restrooms and the water fountain. She beckoned to him with her eyes, and he went to her, politely excusing himself and leaving the reporters with his mother, currently engaged in telling them the intricate details of her earlier relationship with Sam's Dad. A near impossibility given the circumstances, Sam stole a moment alone with

Maggie Haley.

When he got to Maggie, Sam stopped short, not wanting to invade the space that she had set between them the day before. But so much had happened in the meantime.

"Sam?" Maggie spoke first, and she took a step closer. "I'm sorry about yesterday, about everything. I was so hasty and cruel in my words to you. I didn't even give you a chance to speak. To be honest, I couldn't have born hearing you say a word. You would have changed my mind, and I would have had to go against my father, which I'm not ready to do yet. You would have changed my mind so quickly, like you did in the courtroom today. I just know it. And I'm afraid I hurt you on the stand this morning. Can you ever forgive me?"

"Yes," Sam said, unequivocally.

At that moment, the Court's Chief Aide entered the hallway from behind the closed doors of the courtroom and announced, "Please return to the courtroom for the justice's decision."

Sam's eyes met Maggie's. There would be no separation between them from that moment on, despite the limitations of time and space and the folly of events and personalities that have plagued human beings in love from the beginning of time. So be it.

40 – THE DECISION

When all had gathered and had been seated, the justices entered quickly. They had other cases to hear that day in addition to this one. The Chief Justice quickly made her statement to the gallery and to the press:

"We have reached a decision in the preliminary matter of 'Belders, Hatcher, & Dormont v. The State.' It's not often that we hear matters this quickly after they occur, but this is a rare happenstance and required our attending to it. I want to thank all of the local authorities that so expeditiously and expertly got the materials to us and helped in the preparations for convening this session. We have reviewed the entire matter, from the briefs on the case to the transcripts from the testimony today."

"We believe – and I speak for the entire court, though there is some dissension that can be read and understood further by reading the summaries of our individual opinions at the court's website next week – first, that the Downing Schools violated the State laws on the testing system. There is no doubt about this fact. We also believe, second, that the State's penalties were harsh and uncalled for, even though they, too, are called for by law. We are, however, though realizing the lack of seeming balance in our understandings and in our decision, setting aside the actions of the State Department of Education and ruling that the Downing School District be given a year to implement a new curriculum and show this court next summer how it intends to prove that its students have learned a thorough and rich curriculum. This is a call to the district for all grade levels, not just the 8th grade. The previously employed staff is to return to the school, along with all of the students, without prejudice. The school personnel is to have no contact with the State Department of Education, and report only to this court."

"Both Maggie and Sam and all of their friends in Downing deserve to have the best possible education, and part of the determination of what that consists of must be left to local professionals, like school teachers, school administrators, and parents themselves. This is the letter and the spirit of the law as it is embedded in our state constitution, no matter the extent to which it has been ignored in educational law and policy. It is my belief that this decision will draw considerable second-guessing and ire from a multitude of parties. But I don't care, we don't care. We have to do something to reverse the trend of schooling as technical training for God knows what and get back to educating children again for lives as citizens in a democracy. We need to do the hard work of drawing students into interesting, difficult explorations that are intellectual and stimulating and perhaps serve some social good in and of themselves. If we aren't doing that, then whither our education system? Whither our society? I'm afraid that sitting in front of a computer screen all day long doesn't qualify as a good public education. It's time to begin reversing the trend. To the students and parents and teachers in Downing, you have shown us the error of the system and the courage to confront it. We'll take the brunt of the heat from hereon out as a court, and we know that the State Board of Education and the legislature, who are responsible for this mess, will soon be in court arguing with us for a reversal. In the meantime, you get back to the work of teaching and learning. For the next academic year, no data on testing will flow from Downing to the state. We'll hear the results of your experiment on a special court date set for…June next year. This court is adjourned."

The Chief Justice banged her gavel and disappeared with the rest of the justices. The courtroom erupted in applause, and Maggie Haley rushed to Sam and hugged him.

41 – A SHORT CAR RIDE, HOME

After the rush of reporters in the hallway and the race to their waiting cars, the victors piled into a large motor car supplied by Greene and Kilpatrick for the short ride home. The car reminded Betsy Sanders of a limousine she once rode in with Mr. Sanders to a school dance. They all piled in, victors: Betsy, then Sam, then the lawyers, then Belders, Hatcher, Willson, and Dormont. They hugged and whooped and tipped cannisters of celebratory soda pop all the way out of town. When they reached the rural plains surrounding the capital and lying interminably, it seemed, between their small hometown and almost anywhere else, they all fell silent, pacified by the quickly rising and falling excitement of the past two days and the calm ride. After a long silence, Harriet Hatcher spoke first.

"Cindy?" Harriet queried, looking out the window, watching the scattered trees and the corn and cows go by, wandering, "We've known each other a long time. But, I'll never get over the surprise I felt when you first went along with Pete about teaching *Huck Finn*. What made you change your mind so quickly, and support Pete and Sam on this quest? Why didn't you just keep quiet and let this thing play out? The test would have rolled on with one boy missing the test and one teacher knowing, and no-doubt keeping, one of the greatest, best kept secrets."

Cindy met Harriet's eyes when she turned to her, knowing she was opening the door rhetorically, not needing a direct answer; Harriet knew the answer. But Cindy gave it anyway, buoying their dream of a somewhere else, a somewhere new, like Steinbeck's George might chant to Lennie in a time of desperation, or hope, recalling the dream that kept them going. "Harriet, you know I'm not a very complicated person. It's not that hard, really. I had just seen enough of things as they currently are. Just like the Chief Justice, I think that responsible people have let public education slip away from us. We let the state take over. It's ironic, isn't it, that all the while that politicians ran on platforms based on local control, and liberty, and freedom from big government, they created big, centralized government schemes to micro-manage and control public education. While power slipped away from teachers, administrators, and parents in the 1990s, way back, we just sat and watched it happen. It never should have happened. Now look what we let others get us into: Supporting an immoral, unjust educational system based on faulty assumptions about teaching, learning, children, and society. I just decided to be a part of the solution, and not the problem any longer. I merely managed the status quo for so long that I almost forgot what I knew about teaching and learning. Sam Sanders made me remember children, and thinking, and curiosity again. It made me feel good, and alive again. I'd like to feel that way every day I go into school from now on. Perhaps I will. Maybe we will together."

They sat silent for a mile or so, relishing her words; Dormont always proved herself to be eloquent, up to the moment and the question at hand.

Then Dormont herself turned to Pete Willson, "What do you suggest we do now, Pete?"

Without hesitating, Pete said, "I say we go to work on the staff. We have a core of people who understand what we are trying to do. Let's use them as team leaders to teach the others. Let's design a simple means for collecting the students' best work in a format that is readily accessible and can be judged by us and by trusted, outside parties. Let's give the students a chance to design their studies, help them plan major activities and projects, and then go public with their work through presentations and their writing, both along the way and at the end. It's going to be a lot of work, but I've read enough about this approach, and worked closely enough with it last spring and years ago, to know that it can be done and that it can yield. Let's educate all of our students next year so that by the end they are on fire about some topic or issue or subject. Are we anywhere close to being on the same wave length?"

Dormont answered, "We're close, Pete, really close. I like it. I'm appointing you Chair of the reorganizing committee. I want Teddy Hersh to be your Co-Chair. Do you have any problem with that?"

"No, I can work with Teddy Hersh, as long as she doesn't hijack me at the coffee machine, or maybe as long as she does!"

They all chuckled, recalling the story about Teddy's first attack on Pete in the spring once she realized what he was doing with *Huck Finn* in his classes.

Cindy continued, pressing Pete: "How do you feel about the teachers in the upper grades in the school, grades 9-12? They are part of the school staff, after all, and will be working with this group of students that includes Sam. This isn't just an eighth grade 'thing.' All students in all grades will be affected. I want you to lead one of the new ninth grade teams next year, Sam's team."

Pete replied, "Well, this is the thing, I mean, I don't know how they all will react. But the buzz around school was that many teachers in the high school welcomed the potential changes last spring. I think we'll have to pose it to them and see what happens. I'm grateful for the opportunity, Cindy, I'll make the most of it."

"Then it's settled," Dormont responded. "We'll first work with the faculty, and then plan a way to get at the curriculum and teaching questions that we have. Ultimately, we'll have to think and plan hard about assessing student learning in ways that will make the knowledge they have gained public and accessible. Do you think we can do it in so short a time, Sam?"

Sam, excited about his teachers' passion and insight, and riding so close to it, said, "I don't think we have much choice. But based on what I've seen, if anyone can get it done, you all can."

Pete put his hand on Sam's shoulder, claiming him and his generosity, and his quiet confidence.

"That helps a lot, Son," Pete said, and they sped into town, the journey just begun.

42 – STARTING OVER

News spread quickly through town and through the teachers' ranks about the winning day in the capital city. People passed the word like wildfire about opening day for teachers and how much would be at stake. All teachers were to report the following Monday for a full day of discussion and planning for the school year. A full day, of course, didn't seem like much and it wasn't with so much at stake. But Dormont and Willson and others couldn't complain. They had their school back and the opportunity to make something completely new out of the old. Chances like this came around once in a lifetime, they knew, and sometimes never. Their recent brush with the possibility of "sometimes never" as a reality left them grateful for the new opportunities as well as excited and filled with anticipation for Monday.

When Monday came, Dormont and Willson and Hatcher felt ready. They had previously discussed taking an open-ended approach, allowing the teachers to talk about ideas they had for dealing with their new freedom to create curriculum, classroom-based activities, and alternative assessments. They felt as though they couldn't just tell teachers what to do, but that they needed to rely on the expertise and experience of the entire staff to help the whole group take its next steps. Just telling the staff what to do by providing a "how to" set of seminars felt just like putting the same old type of authoritarian, dictatorial system in place that had existed for so long. But how would they get the proper balance between what the teachers knew and had become used to and the professional capacity that each one of them had to truly teach?

They got some feedback from Teddy Hersh that seemed hopeful. She said in a late Sunday afternoon meeting with them that most of the teachers she had talked with seemed supportive and eager for the new challenges. But she also warned that several of the teachers she knew, several of them staunch traditionalists, had suggested that they might try to undermine the new efforts. They wouldn't know until Monday how this might look or play out.

When Monday finally came, the teachers met as usual all together with the administration for a doughnut and hot coffee breakfast before the day's events. It seemed like a smaller crowd than usual because several prominent members of the staff weren't there; this became evident to Cindy near the end of the breakfast when she checked the teacher list against the attendance of the assembled crowd. She noticed that Beech, Harvey, Jarvis, and Bellamy from the high school and that Burden, Brooks, Williams, and Conity weren't there from the middle school. Early childhood teachers James, Sanborn, and Battelle weren't there, either. Cindy counted these 11 from her roster as absent, in all, that hadn't shown up yet. Everyone else on the list was there. To be truthful, she feared the worst, and the clock ticked toward the moments of truth to come.

Dr. Dormont didn't have much time for the fear to take hold, however, because as soon as she looked up from her clipboard she saw all 11 of the missing teachers marching into the gymnasium together, locked arm-in-arm. How strange.

They remained locked arm-in-arm this way as Jarvis stepped to the microphone perched on the temporary dais set up for the day's speakers. She spoke to the members of the assembled crowd of teachers, most still sipping coffee and plowing down doughnuts. But they came to an immediate silence for her. The teachers had seen and experienced a lot the past few months that was out of the ordinary, but this absolutely took the cake. They sensed something monumental about to happen.

"I'm Brandy Jarvis. I have taught 4th grade here in Downing for 22 years. I know most of you, and respect you a great deal. I also know well and respect deeply the colleagues I represent this morning, all of who are standing in front of you, locked arm-in-arm as a show of solidarity. It is our last act as teachers in this school district…"

Another strange buzz raced through the crowd, one of agitation, and excitement. How could this be? Teachers stood in disbelief, turning to each other with their reactions, spontaneously shocked, angered, saddened. They recognized their strong, able colleagues standing in front of them, and knew, at once, that they were gone.

"We believe that the supreme court of this state acted egregiously and with malice towards us at the hearing last week. Many of us witnessed the event in Richway. Quite frankly, we felt that the Chief Justice, by law, had no choice but to find for the state and force us back into the schools in Downing, the schools as we have known them for so long. But her open-ended and irresponsible judgment left us reeling. We have no sympathy for or real understanding of the movement that Dr. Dormont and Pete Willson and Harriet Hatcher and Sam Sanders, for that matter, are trying to lead. We think they constitute the lunatic fringe in educational thought and will not support or participate in any reforms that they espouse. Today we tender our resignations. We wish you the best in your endeavors, though politically we will do our best in whatever walks of life we find ourselves to undo and undermine your work. We think the steps you are about to take are bad for children, bad for teachers, and bad for society. You are taking, essentially, what works and what is proven to be effective educationally, and throwing it out the window for nothing except half-baked theories and promises. We'll have none of it. The moment the state closed down this school district was our last day. Good-bye."

And with that, the group marched out of the gymnasium, to their cars, and down the road to new lives without teaching as they had known it. They would never know the type of teaching that would take root and flourish in this school district. Dormont stood shocked for a moment, and tears actually came to her eyes. But she marched up the stairs of the dias, looked out over the remaining crowd of teachers and administrators, and grabbed the microphone off the floor.

43 – SHOULD I STAY OR SHOULD I GO?

Cindy spoke to the remaining teachers and school staff:

"Please, everyone, take a seat, a last doughnut or two and some fresh coffee, and then let's get on with it." Her steady, strong demeanor held them together and reassured so many. It became evident to all, though, that tears continued to roll down her cheeks as she spoke. Harriet handed her a tissue. She accepted it.

The crowd shuffled around a bit, still rather shocked by Jarvis and her group's antics, and pretty quickly seated themselves. Nobody else, it seemed, had thoughts of going anywhere.

Cindy looked out over the group a few times. The pregnant pause made the teachers burst with anticipation. They needed her, desperately, to set things straight and provide some direction.

"Listen," she brushed away the last tear from her lower cheek, "You know what this school means to me. You know, I hope, what you mean to me as individual people. You are my colleagues and friends. So were they. And they still are, though they may not be willing to reciprocate that same feeling for awhile." The teachers laughed nervously back, mostly to help her out through this tough moment.

"But I'm so proud and filled with hope regarding your participation in today's planning session and activities and the opening of school. I'm most impressed with your willingness to return and to enter into something that is completely new to so many of you. But I want to send out one last invitation, along with a warning, right now, to every last one of you: If you aren't in this for the long-haul, all the way through the end of the year, then you better follow them right out the door. This isn't going to work for children or with us if you aren't 'in.' Of course, this doesn't mean that you can't disagree, or that you won't have different ideas about what we should be doing. Of course you will and you should. What I'm saying is you have to take on the spirit and the energy for more authentic teaching and learning among students and your peers. If you don't want to explore what that might look like and how we might become better teachers and learners together, then you must go now. Please, just go now."

With that last sentence, Cindy looked each one of the remaining teachers in the eye and kept her arm up and her index finger pointed out the side door that the Jarvis Crowd had just exited. No one moved a muscle.

She repeated, "Speak now, or forever hold your peace…"

Not a twitch, even with her excellent use of some twisted marital humor.

"Now, quite honestly, I'm tired of speeches. We have been hearing them for several months. I don't know where they have gotten us, but at least we know where people stand. I know that you are staying. Now, I have to go out and find 11 teachers to fill 11 vacancies. I will no doubt be calling on all of you to help lessen the load as we reel new, willing people in. It might be hard to find them quickly. While I'm working on that problem, Pete Willson and Teddy Hersh will be directing today's activities with you. Have at it."

Dr. Dormont walked off the stage. Strangely, spontaneously, the first row rose to applaud her. The entire faculty gave her a standing ovation as she exited the gym. The teachers kept clapping, willing themselves into the future with energy, and passion.

44 – BRASS TACKS

Teddy Hersh watched Dr. Dormont exit, looked at Pete, gave him a touch on the hand, and made her way up front. She took her turn at the microphone.

"Okay, I'm staying. I haven't really been sold on any of this from the beginning, but I do recognize the spirit and the courage and the possibilities in this is staff and student body. So let's get on with it. Here's how we'll start the day. It's time to get down to brass tacks, let's get this thing going, wherever it takes us. We're all in it for the long haul. We have a list of groups of about five people each that will work on curriculum ideas and choose activities and materials for the first three weeks of class. I'm passing the list around now," she handed the papers to aides who began distributing the list sheets.

"Let's be sure and use the expertise of Ms. Hatcher to track down the materials we'll need. Some of the stuff we want might be hard to find so let's give her all the leeway and time that we can. Further, all of the standard subject areas are represented in each group (Language Arts and Math), so we're hoping for a more integrated approach to the curriculum you design. Your task, therefore, is to come up with a sketch of the next three-week period. Remember, for some of us, all the old familiar rules are off. Go with it, and listen to the team leaders. At the end of the day, let's share those sketches with each other and see how much progress we've made. Each Friday for the next several weeks, we'll dismiss early and spend the remainder of the day reflecting on the just completed week and planning ahead for the next week. Okay? ... Let's go then, time's a wastin'."

The teachers milled around, finding their groups. Most of them had never worked on the curriculum before because the test-focused curriculum for 20 years came packaged in computer programs from the state and directly into the students' individual terminals for study. No teacher in this group had ever had anything to say about the curriculum. No one had ever used a book in class, save for last year's brief experiment in the middle school with *Huck Finn*. Many of the teachers had no personal relationship since their work took place only in isolated classrooms under very precise and controlled conditions. For three decades, there had been no reason for teachers to talk together about students or the curriculum. These topics were moot.

Obviously, then, most of the groups would struggle with first steps. It was the role of the team leaders, chosen quickly but on purpose by Dormont and Pete and Teddy, who would provide the initial leadership and guidance for making the groups work.

Pete's new group included other ninth grade teachers. Dr. Dormont thought it would be a good idea for Pete to move to the high school with Sam's class. Mary Baldwin and Jerry Strigent from Math and Bert Convoyan and Jean Bontollin from Language Arts made up the group with Pete. They were charged to work with 100 students in the ninth grade. Other five person teams would work with students groups of about 100 through all of the high school levels. This group showed, just like the others, that the hardest thing to do was to get started. No one knew what to say, not even Pete, who stalled, milling around getting a last doughnut and coffee and then nervously shuffling papers while the group members settled into their seats around the round table.

So Jean Bontollin started things off. "Listen, I really don't know where to begin. But maybe I can offer a suggestion. Since the math folks probably don't know much about what we've been doing in Language Arts and vice versa, perhaps I can start by telling where we've been, where we'd like to go, and how we think that might be possible. What do you think?"

"Sure, sure, go ahead Jean, really, …" they all offered unanimously and simultaneously.

"Well, okay then, first off, I've been helping students learn the writing and reading skills block for ninth graders for 15 years. I see the prompts on the computer screen and help students with the exercises sometimes. The basic units are creating the thesis statement, then developing supporting evidence or arguments to support the main point(s), and finally editing/grammar. Students are strictly confined to expository writing. Second, I support students' reading units by reading along and answering their questions, as they are posed through the computer. Whether or not students get the content of the articles or stories always gets evaluated through 'objective' tests or quizzes given at the end of the reading. I never, ever ask students questions or delve into deeper discussion about the readings with the students. This has never been forbidden, really, but it has always been a practice frowned upon in teacher education programs and penalized through teacher evaluations over the years."

"Very interesting, Jean," said Jerry. "I think you'll find we have a lot in common in the Mathematics area. We don't do problem sets with students by giving an example and then assigning examples to work out. I understand that teachers used to do that in the 20th century; that approach offered at least some amount of critical thinking and human exchange, though I understand quite a few Math teachers advocated for a more problem-solving and critical thinking approach to math even back then. Nowadays, students get a brief recorded video prompt about the skill or problem to be solved and then they get endless drill in solving the same problem type over and over again. This format is used for addition and subtraction all the way through calculus. It's mind numbing really, and most of our students don't progress in math because they get stuck in the mastery sets well below their ability levels because they need more help in learning concepts. We just don't have the opportunity to work with individual students when they need it, and quite frankly, I don't have the skills to help students work the more conceptual math problems myself. I'd need to learn the maths right along with my students if I were to leave the computer behind, which is essentially what we are deciding to do. I'm nervous about it, and really don't know where to even begin."

Pete realized that the group had its work cut out for it. He wondered if there was any hope that the group could progress past their meager, collective pasts as teachers and forge new professional lives together.

45 – SOMETHING NEW

A very long silence ensued...

Then Pete Willson gave it a try.

"Listen, Jean and Jerry, really, that's all very helpful from a subject area perspective. Most of us know what has been going on with the computer-assisted curriculum in language arts and math, that it has been boring and shallow. The grade level, to me, or the subject areas we know something about make little difference now, though. What makes a difference to me is that we get back to teaching. I realize that we have been licensed by the state to teach certain subjects. But we really haven't been teaching them anyway, and we really don't know that much about them in the first place. Instead, we first and foremost have to play a role as human beings in the lives of the children in our school. That means that we have to communicate with them, and that the curriculum we design has to be communicative and relational. The content has to have something to do with children's lives, and the experience and the results of their learning ought to be real, somehow authentic, and perhaps socially valuable to them and the publics they represent."

"Are you saying," asked Bert, "that we should ask the students what it is they want to learn about?" He chuckled to himself, mocking Pete.

Pete offered back quickly: "Let me tell you about a few things I've been reading. Some of it is pretty old, to some of you, perhaps, ancient history. I know Teddy Hersh felt this way til just a few weeks ago. John Baton wrote a book in the 1990s called *Integrating Curriculum*. In it he claimed that students, if given the opportunity, can voice their concerns about the world and their lives, and with guidance actually design projects that will help address those concerns. These concerns, questions, images, or themes are called 'organizing centers,' and once students start working on them they develop deep knowledge about the subject areas as well as social knowledge about each other and their communities. I'm thinking that if we are going to do this right, ultimately by asking students to take charge of their own learning and invest in it and have something more than a test score at the end of the year to show what they have learned, then they really ought to be involved with the curriculum, not just passive receivers of it. Bottom line: even if we remake a curriculum that introduces students to real books and interactive processes, what good is it if it's still something we are merely doing *to* them, not *with* them?"

Mary's face knotted up. "You think we should ask the students what it is they want to learn? They know less than we do about how to think things through, how to ask questions. They don't know the first thing."

"You see, Mary, that's where I think you're wrong, that's where all of us have been wrong for decades. These kids, they know stuff. They're smart. They have lives. They have deep questions. We just don't pay any attention, or even ask in the first place. I saw it last year in my *Huck Finn* seminars. These kids have practically no experience working this way in school, and yet they still hunger for discourse, for debate, for exchanging ideas. And for some reason, fiction and other forms of writing still have a way of energizing them. We have been so busy building a machine to control them six hours a day, including brainwashing you with a teacher 'education' to believe they are stupid, that we've lost sight of how intelligent they are. Sam Sanders is just the tip of the iceberg. Last spring during these *Huck Finn* seminars with eighth graders I had to pinch myself at times in order to prove that what I was seeing and hearing from them wasn't a dream, but a true reality. Thinking, real thinking, happening in my classroom, and out loud."

The rest of the team looked back at Pete blankly. Instead of stopping, heartbroken and shocked at their apathy, he continued.

"Listen, here's what I suggest we do to start. Let's ask the students what they are concerned about. We'll do that in a session with all 100 of them together in the morning the first day. We'll break into homeroom groups and design one project with the students to work on together the first four weeks. The project will have social and academic knowledge attached to it. Each morning, let's work on subject area knowledge that we think might inform their projects and that also addresses what we think and know 9th graders ought to be learning and doing. This will require that we read more widely, even in the sciences and the social studies, which went out of style 15 years ago but nonetheless have some bearing today. Then in the afternoon, let's let them work on their projects, use the media center, and work with townspeople and their areas of expertise to inform their work. At the end, let's have the students give a presentation of what they learned and how they think that learning can have an impact on some problem or institution here in Downing. Let's invite everyone from around the area, including people like Missy Tallons from the *Record-Star*, to see what we are doing and to spread the word that education is back and that rote learning and test taking are out in Downing…"

Silence.

"Come on, what do you say? What do we have to lose?" implored Pete.

"I'm in," said Jenny, "but you need to know this is completely new ground for all of us. None of us is used to working this hard. We have no idea what to expect from students. We are going to need help and support from you and Dormont and the parents and everybody, or it's going to be a disaster. Can you guarantee the support?"

"I'm here and I'm not going anywhere. You've got it Jenny," said Pete.

"I'm in, too, then," offered Mary and Jerry, shifting uncomfortably in their seats.

They all looked at Bert.

"What? What are you all looking at? You know I'm in, just have to give Willson a hard time periodically. If he's going to be some kind of 'caped crusader of curriculum' around here then he needs to have a villain to crush. You all know I'm here because I need this job and that I loved the teaching job I *used to have*. But if this is what it takes to keep the job, and you all are crazy enough to buy this rigarmoroll, then I guess I have no choice but to say, 'okay.'"

For a moment Pete knew they would make it, though the road there would be filled with fits and starts and no doubt worse.

PART THREE:

SAM SANDERS SCHOOL

46 – SWIMMING UPSTREAM

Missy Tallons here. Well, it's been awhile since I've weighed in, but it's time for me to do so. Framing this last movement of the story is, I think, critical for the whole story to make sense to the reader. It's a complicated task putting all of this together in a form that is digestible; I'm sure you'll be able to make sense of it now that I think I actually understand what happened in Downing.

I've been reflecting lately on the fact that reporters see so much in a day's time and a lifetime that often reveals the underside of human life. Over time I've gotten to report several human-interest stories that have been uplifting, but usually I only get to see the bad stuff since the news industry just looks for the negative, typically. That's probably why I have found the assignment of tracking the changes in the Downing Schools so intriguing and life-changing.

I have seen so much that is positive come from the work that the school and the community have done together to make Downing a virtual throwback, a public school system claiming the content and practices of the best 20th century schools before they went out of style right along with the popularity and functionality of the gasoline powered car and democracy, as we knew them then. It's easy for me to say, in retrospect, that all citizens over 50 years of age as of 2025 truly missed an opportunity to stem the tide of government oppression over schools way back when; it's even easier for me to say, after seeing Downing in action, that we can reclaim some critical ground, and perhaps even have our schools back, by looking closely at how schools can work and how teachers and students can create a place that works together.

But we have to reject the notions that standardization of curriculum and assessment in any way reflect our deepest values, and that teaching can be done just as well by a machine as by a human being. These assumptions led us down a certain path; we now have a chance to cut a new trail.

This project, of seeing this through, will take enormous will and sacrifice, though; I wonder if we have enough of these qualities as a people to go around. I wonder if we have enough ideas and vocabulary to defend and describe just what it is we mean by providing a good public education for every citizen as part of our civic and moral responsibility to each other. I wish we could bottle what the Downing people have, especially the teachers and other school people at the site, and give it as an antidote to the passive "stand by idly and watch the demise of schooling" attitudes we have displayed as a people as a whole over the years. As several of the protagonists in this story have told me over and again the past year or so, only time will tell. As I see it, time is running out. What the public schools can give us is immeasurable, but we have to move them past the shallow, dictatorial, controlling institutions that they for the most part have become in the late 2020s.

It's just truly amazing what can happen in a short time in schools when the energies of the intellect are unleashed. The classrooms and people and events I report here all approximate what I saw in Downing. I focus on several teachers and their work in the story because I spent so much time with them. But this doesn't mean that every one transformed themselves and their work in the same ways at the same time or that it was easy. Going down the right path can sometimes be very difficult, even devastating. What I am claiming, and what I mean, is that the picture I paint here is accurate, and probably suggests that the types of things that were going on across the schools, since the teachers were collaborating and sharing at unprecedented levels, at least in comparison with their lifetimes of experiences in public schools, revolutionized their work and how they see what they do as teachers as a different enterprise than before.

This is the end of their story for now, though just the beginning, really. Ultimately, this story needs to show the reader how the teachers, students, and school became the type of school that the Supreme Court Justices in Richway might call "excellent."

47 – TWO WEEKS DOWN

The fledgling ninth grade team of Pete Willson and Jean Bontollin (Language Arts) and Mary Baldwin, Bert Convoyan, and Jerry Strigent (Mathematics) kept meeting all through the first two weeks of school. After their tepid start, they started clicking together, learning more about each other and how each other thought, though once in a while they had personal interactions that strained them. At the beginning, the lessons they taught and the content they covered with students didn't overlap very much. They were very traditional, focusing on teacher talk and teacher knowledge and rote exercises by the students.

The teachers, even those in teams, still operated in merely parallel, very separate universes within the walls of this small school community. Just like during all of their previous years together, they didn't share much across classrooms and experiences with students or together. That was all slowly changing, and about to change more drastically.

Pete kept at it, constantly encouraging the team members to talk together more about how the work they were doing in classrooms to deeply engage their students did more than merely overlap. How did the teaching and the curriculum connect? What themes seemed to resonate across classrooms and materials? What decisions could they make together to highlight similar, connected knowledge, ideas, and themes so that the students could see connections and build their own new knowledge bases?

On Friday after school, at the end of the second week, the team sat and reflected together in Pete's classroom, now transformed from a machine-based environment into a person-based environment. Instead of computer terminals all around, large round tables with chairs – with ample room on the tables for writing with paper and pen or an old laptop computer – dominated the center of the room. Supporting technology, like writing terminals with printers and actual paper, dotted the perimeter.

Pete asked, innocently enough after a few minutes of hot coffee banter, "Bert, what kinds of math operations are students working on next week?"

"I don't see how that's any of your business, really, Willson. What difference does it make to you concerning what *my* students are doing? Just stick to English," Bert Convoyan flipped back.

Undaunted, Pete shot back: "It makes every difference in the world, Bert, since they aren't just *your* students. They are *our* students, we all teach them. And knowledge doesn't come in mere isolated bits, unless we decide to do it that way. We have actually decided *not* to do it that way."

Pete felt like he had to respond pointedly to Bert to stem any tide of negativity, though as he spoke he felt his internal temperature rise, and he didn't like that feeling. He, like the others, teetered emotionally on the edge, dog-tired from the week just behind them; he continued with measured words, in control, gathering himself, masking his anger.

"I'm unwilling to parse the students out only as mathematicians or writers or lab technicians for certain periods during the day anymore. They might be all of these things, all at the same time. What matters is what they are working on together, and what it is that they bring to the table and want to build on. I also want every day to be meaningful and for us to take advantage of opportunities to connect what we are doing across classrooms. Now, we have been talking about building this first thematic unit around the themes of 'equity' and 'justice.' Does each person we study or phenomenon in the world that we are looking at connect with notions of equal opportunity and social justice, in reality and under the actual law? So I'm just curious if anything you are working on might connect, that's all. Because if it doesn't connect, we ought not to be doing it."

Pete's pointed comments silenced Bert, but Bert simmered, his eyes darting from person to person to pick up their reactions. Bert didn't answer. Mary's, and Jerry's, and Jean's eyes mostly looked down at their own notebooks and not up at him. But finally after a pregnant pause, Mary looked up, and then and directly at Bert, though their eyes did not meet.

Her voice trembled just a bit.

"Bert, for this to work you have to buy into it. We can't go back in time in ways that are liberating for us and for students if we have to constantly fight with you. It would be one thing if you were offering critique and productive conflict through questions and concerns. But you're just mean, and you've gotten meaner every day from the beginning. I want you to stop it, right now, or at least start by telling us what's bothering you."

Her conviction resonated with the others, jarring them from their Friday afternoon fatigue. They looked up, no doubt gaining strength from her words, and looked at Bert. Their eyes pleaded for a response from him. He didn't have to give in, he just needed to acknowledge them and what they wanted from him: cooperation.

48 – BERT ON BOARD, FOR NOW

"All right, all ready… You don't have to get all huffy about it," saving face a bit with his gruff, though acquiescent comeback. Bert continued, after a significant pause and a considerable amount of nervous thumb-twiddling. "I'm actually going to explore some statistics with the students, working on some initial ideas about probability, and incorporating some rather simple algebraic equations with these ideas."

"Cool," offered Pete in his best 1980s schtick, and as sincerely as could be in an attempt to diffuse the tension, "because I'm looking at some late 20th century poetry on the environment, and Jerry is taking a leap with a science experiment he has been wanting to work on with the students. What are you planning, Jerry?"

"Well," he offered while thinking on his response, "I'm taking a look at water sampling techniques and thought that we'd take samples from several sources including the retaining pond down by the plant, the river, and Morse Lake. I'm teaching the students to look for extreme cases of pollution, like the creation of conditions of impurity in water supplies, given our history here, though I'm not quite sure that I can find right the materials for the work like collection tubes and the like…"

Jerry paused for a few moments, sizing up his confession, "Quite frankly, I haven't done much science since I myself was *in* the fourth grade, way back in the 1980s, let alone taught anything on the subject."

They all chuckled, remembering that they each had studied other subject areas before math and language arts became kings for three decades.

Jerry continued, "I had a grades 9-12 certification to teach science years ago, but that converted over to math and language arts just like everybody else's. There just wasn't much use for teaching science in schools, you know. Remember that thinking? It was only for the 'elite' students preparing for the university and destined to be engineers and scientists, and they only took these 'mysterious' science courses once they got to college. I remember what the scientific method is, but I'm learning science from the ground up, with my students. I think it will be exciting, but the learning curve will be steep."

Jean offered, "I'd be willing to help you, Jerry. Why don't we take double periods out on the collection activity, back-to-back, so they have more time to collect the samples, mark them adequately, and begin analyzing them?"

"That would be great," Jerry replied.

Mary Baldwin offered, "And I'd like to look at the social implications of our own industrial plant, its impact on the environment and on the social dynamics of Downing. I know that social studies was a big part of the curriculum back in the

1990s before testing and the computer-based curriculum took most of the contro-versy and ideas out of teaching and learning. Our students have experience with social issues, and school ought to be a place to explore them more deeply together. I'll work on this as your science experiments, poetry, and statistics take shape with the project. It's invigorating to work day-to-day with the students developing the curriculum. The materials I bring in are almost always complemented by something the students have concerns over or want to share. I won't have any problem moving along with you and the students as you need me. Just keep me posted on insights and developments in your classrooms best you can."

Pete summed up: "Awesome, I think we're making progress. This doesn't work without each of us playing a part, and communicating together. Our students can do it if we can. That's probably the biggest challenge."

They laughed nervously with Pete while he got out the master schedule for the team and they began planning further. Their bodies moved closer to the center of the table, as they talked and laughed and planned.

They were becoming a team, all the while knowing that pulling Bert in would be a continuous project, and that at any moment he could turn on them.

49 – MAGGIE'S KISS

In the hallway after school, Sam and Maggie stood at their lockers side-by-side and did their best to curtail their passions for each other, not wanting too much for others to catch on and tease, though teen-age romance wouldn't have proven anything new to their peers. They just felt self-conscious, and unsure about the whole thing, though their feelings proved undeniable when they got close to each other, when Sam moved the hair back from Maggie's eyes or touched the underside of her forearm gently.

"You coming by the house tonight, Sam? I'd like to work on our science project. Let's get some advance water samples to test before the field trip," Maggie asked as seriously as she could, though she couldn't mask the teasing, inviting grin curling at her lips.

"You just want to taunt your dad with me, don't you girl?" Sam shot back, his wicked, pointed wit catching her, but nowhere near off-guard.

"Yes, I would, but if you want to play like that, and not talk 'science' with me, maybe the invitation isn't as good as it was a minute ago," she said turning back to her locker, pulling books out now and dumping them into her bag as carefully and quickly as she could, feigning a quick getaway.

"Oh, I'm plenty interested in science, all right. 7 o'clock okay?" Sam asked as nonchalantly as he could, trying to regain ground, recovering as skillfully as he could, letting on that he cared not to be too distant, knowing full well the game they were playing was courtship sparring at its best, pulling them closer together. Sam loved Maggie's spirit.

"Great. But make sure you're on time, we'll only have an hour or so before daddy'll start hunting us down at 8," she wheeled past him, touching him lightly on his arm and then pinching his elbow, which turned him around toward her. Now they were face-to-face, awkwardly so.

And then she kissed Sam on the cheek. Sam had no chance to kiss her back even if he had thought of it, her kiss came so quickly. Flustered, he just sighed after her, his voice trailing off loud enough for her to hear, "See ya."

And Maggie was off, down the hallway with friends, laughing and mixing in as naturally as could be.

Left standing alone with his own racing thoughts, not only about Maggie Haley but about science class as well, Sam tried to pull himself together so he would take home the things he needed to complete his studies for the next day. Like the rest of his peers, Sam found some degree of excitement and newfound responsibility in preparing for class. For years, all he had done is show up for school. He read books on his own, but never anything that was assigned by a teacher for a class because it provided necessary background for a lesson being taught or for a project being pursued. This was all different ground, and worth covering.

He figured he was steady enough to move after a few moments. Maggie had certainly caught him off guard, and nearly knocked his legs out from under him.

50 – SCIENCE CONTENT

As a result of Sam's ascension to 9th grade, his mom made sure that he would have a way to get around town and to school that fit the life of a high school student – so she asked Pete to restore an old, beat up 1992 bright yellow Ford Mustang. An ancient pile of rubble at the beginning of its rebirth, Willson worked all summer while the Sanders were gone to put it back in shape. Sam learned to drive it pretty quickly, he'd been driving tractors and such around the farm for years anyway and had driven battery powered cars with a license since he was 13, so it didn't take long to get it on the road after Willson brought it by. The car ran on gasoline, not electricity like modern cars, so Sam stayed tied rather closely to Pete, who had a gas supplier visit him every month or so to fill a large tank that he used to dispense his own gas at his own house.

The car made Sam feel independent, though his mother had a laundry list of rules for driving that he must follow closely: no driving over 45 miles per hour, no passing, no night driving (yet), etc. The car made him feel cool, too, since nobody at school had anything like it. Lots of kids had never even seen a gas powered car before, except for Willson's dilapidated pickup truck. Sam didn't really have to worry about attaining or keeping any "cool" quotient with the other students as a result of all the publicity and notoriety he had received last school year, and as a result of dating Maggie Haley, who herself carried a lot of influence with her peers. But time goes fast at 15, and things change, and positions and status and confidence can be fleeting. Sam made sure not to show off, but he made no apologies for moving ahead and enjoying his life despite all that had happened.

Sam decided to stop off at Willson's after school to get a little gas and chit-chat with him. When he got to Willson's little ranch on the outskirts of town, he pulled up and pumped 10 quick liters. Sam wrote down how much he had taken on a chart Willson left by the pump for him to fill out when he stopped by for gas. Willson just liked keeping track of things, as far as Sam knew; Willson never presented anyone, his mom especially or Sam himself, with a gas bill, even with gas costs at a prohibitive $5.00 a liter. Sam was beginning to reap the material benefits of Willson's interest in his mother. As far as he was concerned, this was all a bonus. Nothing could be better than it was for Sam at home personally with his mom or with Maggie, except if he had his dad back, but he knew that couldn't happen.

Just as he had finished pumping the gas, Willson came barreling onto the driveway and screeched to a stop right next to Sam. He hopped out to help out.

"Hey, partner, how you doin'? Need a hand?"

"Nah, I'm pretty good, Pete. I got it. Thanks for the gas."

"Don't mention it, Sam. There's more where that came from. And besides, nothing beats seeing you prowl around in that old Mustang. Makes me remember the good ol' days myself…Say, how's it going with your science project?"

"Well, I'm just getting started on it really. We have the water samples to collect tomorrow as a class, and, as I understand it, several experiments to conduct on them. Maggie and I are going down to the river-bed and the lake later to take a few advanced samples. Ms. Belders has a book at the library she's holding for me called *Amateur Chemists at Work in the Community*. Inside it has all these experiments you can conduct on liquid samples at home using everyday chemicals to test for acidity and pollutants and such. We figured since we hadn't done this before that we might take a shot at figuring some things out ahead of time. We need to learn more about the science, tap into the content a little bit."

"Are you figuring each other out a little bit, too?" Pete asked now with a sly little grin curling at his check.

"That's really embarrassing, you know, coming from an old 'has been' like you. Just pay attention to your own love-life problems," Sam playfully shot back.

"I'll stay off your back, Bud. I'm taking your mom out to eat to-night, we're thinking about Max's Palace. You want to bring Maggie?"

"Nah," Sam said as he ducked down into the driver's seat of the Mustang, "You guys go on ahead and have fun. I'm going to Maggie's at 7 and I'll pick something up to eat after the library. I'm going to see Ms. Belders now. She's holding that book."

"Go on then, get out of here, boy," Pete smacked the front hood of Sam's car playfully, a warm send off. They waved fondly, like old friends.

51 – BRIDGE OVER TROUBLED WATERS

Sam rolled down Main Street toward the library. He always slowed to take a look at old man Stevens' place, quiet now, typically, as a result of Stevens serving 25 years in prison with no chance of parole for attempted murder on Sam last spring. Sam just felt curious, deep down, and strangely sad about all that had happened. In this day and age, the trial of a violent criminal like Stevens took very little time. The judge convicted Stevens on the arresting police officer's testimony alone; the trial lasted less than one afternoon and Stevens went away. Sam had barely even thought about it lately. "Out of sight, out of mind," he had supposed. Stevens turned 80 last year; he'd no doubt die in jail. Men often lived to 90 years old these days, but not to 95, 100, or 105. He'd never see Stevens again, a huge relief.

Sam noticed several trucks at Stevens' house, with movers working briskly to take what looked like everything out of the house. He also noticed one of those old time metal signs in the yard that read "Stevens Family Auction, Saturday at Noon by The Wendell Daughters' Auction House. Everything must go!" No doubt Stevens needed the cash for paying off lawyers and keeping the plant going. In his place, Stevens' brother Mike had taken over the everyday finances and management of the plant and had gotten production going again after what seemed like a long lay-off. In reality, it was only about three weeks. But most people felt glad to get back to work. Not many people could go very long without working and still make ends meet. People, generally, had basically hated Stevens, though his plant kept the town and its residents going financially. He was, simply put, a proud, egocentric, mean-spirited, smart, cheating, rich old man who happened to control the purse strings of the whole town.

As he rolled down the block in front of the library, Sam noticed Ms. Belders accepting a cardboard box, open at the top and overflowing with papers, from a man that looked like he was from the same moving company as the guys down the street moving Stevens out.

Sam greeted the man on the steps with a "Good day, Sir" and quickly bounded up to the top, squeezing through the library's front door just closing behind Ms. Belders. When he got all the way inside, he found Ms. Belders at her circulation counter already leafing through the box of papers.

"Whachya got there, Ms. B? The secret papers of Harry Stevens?"

Startled, and a bit distant, she replied, "Oh, Sam, you surprised me. Well, yes, I think maybe they are, Sam," turning toward him, pale faced, strangely frightened now, "Look here, so many of these files have your dad's name on them. And look inside the files. It's all chemistry equations. What do you make of this?"

Sam glanced through the files and found her to be right, file after file said "Sanders: Chemistry" on them. Sam didn't even know his dad knew any chemistry, let alone liked it, or was able to carry on a conversation in it as a language in and of itself. But he could tell that some of the writing, unmistakably, belonged to his father. On many of the pages, it looked as if someone would write one thing, then another person in another hand would add on. It looked like two people carrying on a complex, mysterious conversation in chemistry. As they examined the box and its contents, Ms. Belders found a small envelope attached to the box, "Oh, look, a letter...It's addressed to me," Ms. Belders ripped a letter off the side of the box, attached there by an old piece of scotch tape.

She read it out loud:

Dear Ms. Belders, These documents are critical to understanding the demise of Paul Sanders, my partner and nemesis of so many years. Perhaps you'll make sense of them someday and understand more about what happened to him, why he had to die. These documents are meant to provide pain for his family, since they are basically indecipherable and will lead to years of misunderstanding. But the truth of the matter lies herein and you'll discover it soon enough. There is no other way to the truth but through these documents. Since I'll be gone forever anyway, I'm just glad to cause this last bit of pain and suffering. It will be especially gratifying that those kids at the high school will be wasting part of their school careers trying fruitlessly to figure the mystery out. They'll never get it in a million years, the idiots. Harold Stevens

"Sam, I'm so sorry. Stevens must have known I'd accept these papers and try to make sense of them and show them to you. But I don't know anything about chemistry. And I'm so sorry you heard those nasty words, so soon after your dad and the shooting and all. Will you forgive me?"

"Ms. Belders, you saved my life in this place. I would have gone crazy without you, this place, these books. I'm glad you gave me this information. Maybe it will help us figure out what happened to dad, once and for all. But Stevens called dad his 'partner' and referred to his death as 'why he had to die.' I don't get it; Dad was never Stevens' partner and I thought he died in a car accident."

Ms. Belders pulled Sam to her again, and held him. He was shocked, suddenly aware that the story of his life had a deep, dark side to it.

"We'll get to the bottom of this honey. We will. I promise."

52 – SIFTING, SORTING, STACKING

Belders and Sanders were together again, this time not across the book counter, but side-by-side sifting and sorting through Stevens' strange box of files. Minutes turned to hours as they sat there, weaving through. They didn't get hungry or search for something to drink. Sam finally looked up at the clock and saw the time approaching 7 pm. He had to be at Maggie's by 7 pm, so he put the brakes on their project and asked, "Ms. Belders, where do you think these files are going? What's this all about? I have to go in a few minutes, and just don't want to leave things undone like this."

Very easily, Belders gave her opinion: "Well, it's fairly easy to see that Stevens was a maniac, keeping records like this on file for so long in his house, secreted away. They are no doubt significant and must hold the key to some lock, some secret meaning that is stored here that will shed light on just what the relationship between your dad and Stevens was. He said in his letter that your dad was his 'partner.' I don't remember Paul ever saying anything about that or giving any indication that they were partners of any sort. From what I can see, many, many of the pages are variations of the same things, a conversation about a formula. If you'll look at these two pages, dated March 15, 2009, and March 22, 2009, you see the slight variation. The key, I think, without being a chemist myself, is the introduction of this one new element to the equation and heat being added to the recipe...here," she pointed directly at the last dated archive.

"Do you see the difference, Sam? These are the latest two documents in the whole set by date and notice, here, the red circles around the element and the word heat at the bottom. This must have been some sort of breakthrough they hit upon together."

"Yes, I see," answered Sam, even more curious, "So, what do you think it means?"

"I don't know," puzzled Belders, sure that an answer would come but knowing full well that only time would yield it, "But let's sleep on it and see what we think about it tomorrow. Maybe that will help."

She stood up and started putting the files back in the box while Sam got ready to go.

"Thanks, Ms. Belders. I'll be back tomorrow."

"I know, Sam. See you then. In the meantime, study hard."

"I will," and off he went, noting that his book bag felt a little heavier than usual. Outside on the steps, he stopped and looked inside and saw the chemistry book that Ms. Belders had promised, *Amateur Chemists at Work in the Community.*

53 – A ROTTEN, STINKING HOLE IN THE GROUND

When Sam got to Maggie's house, she was waiting on the porch for him. She ran to the car and jumped in, only a few minutes of daylight left in the day. She had been working on her reading assignment for the next day and helping her mother with dinner. She brought Sam an apple salvaged from the dinner bowl.

"Hey, thanks for the apple," Sam said, devouring it almost immediately.

"You are such a pig, you could at least say 'hi' first," Maggie answered.

"Oh, 'hi,' I know, but I know that you know that I meant to say 'hi,' I'm just hungry, really hungry, and you knew I would be or you wouldn't have brought me the apple, right?"

"Watch it, Sanders. You're being way too cute, now. Listen, we have a mission don't we? Let's get on it. Oh, and my dad says have me home by 8 pm. He keeps asking why you don't come to the door, too."

"I'll come to the door next time, I promise…To the river?"

"Sure you will…To the river."

Maggie pulled out a series of glass jars she had salvaged from the family basement. Her mother told her that they had been used long ago to "can" tomatoes from their garden and that they would be good for collecting and sealing water samples for their science project.

On the way to the river they passed Stevens' plant, pumping away, belching steam from its chimneys and generating a pretty loud racket. Miles away, at the nicest spot in the Mule River that ran right by the plant and by most of the homes in Downing, Maggie and Sam got out of the car, took off their shoes, and waded a foot or two past the bank of the river and out into the cold streaming flow. Their toes about froze. They had gotten so used to the rank smell of the river over time that they barely noticed its rancid odor.

Bending over, tipping her glass jar into the water, which now had begun to smell terribly as it washed against her clothes and stuck to her, Maggie asked, "So where were you? I called your house but your Mom thought you were with me."

"I was at the library. This afternoon Ms. Belders got a box from Stevens' house, delivered from his house right to the library door. It was filled with documents about my dad and a letter to her. For some reason, Stevens is bent on making sure that our family is tortured sufficiently. It had all of these chemistry papers in there, and we were trying to understand what they were all about." He drew two or three jars full of water and placed them in a plastic bag after tightening each lid.

"Chemistry? Sounds like our project is taking shape at just the right time. We're going to have to use chemistry to figure out what is and isn't in this water, right?"

"Right, I think. Since we don't know any chemistry, we're going to have to figure out where to start. Maybe the book Ms. Belders found for us is a place we can start."

"Let's go," she teased, having filled her last jar, and pulling at his elbow while he tried to finish his. "Get that thing filled and carry me out of this water."

"Okay, princess, you got it," Sam held the plastic bag and at the same time whisked Maggie off her feet, as if saving her from a rising torrent or carrying her over a threshold.

"Sam, I had no idea you were so strong," she complimented.

"I'm not," Sam shot back, "But adrenaline, I've found out, can really work wonders. Except, it can make you....clumsy!"

And in that moment Sam had dumped her in the water, on purpose. They splashed and cavorted. Quickly they realized they had to recover all the jars, so they checked to see that they hadn't broken them, then they ran to the car to warm up. They got cold fast in the cool evening breeze and running water. They didn't smell very good, either. Their drinking water tasted okay and all, but it had been rigorously filtered and treated. Everyone knew that the river water was rotten on its own, tainted for decades by Stevens' plant on the river. But technology had made this a rather moot point, they all thought.

"I thought you'd never drop me," Maggie said to Sam in the car, knowing full well he'd done it on purpose, and moving in close to take him by the arm and share his body heat.

"I thought you'd never *drop me, either,*" said Sam back, referring to the summer before and the weeks he had lost her during the trial, not to the splashing episode.

"Good one," Maggie shot back. "Listen to me, Sam Sanders, don't worry about me. I'm not going anywhere."

"Good, because I'm afraid I'm going to need a good friend through all of this."

She put her head on his shoulder and he drove back to town with the smartest, most beautiful girl he'd ever known. These qualities made her rank odor appear minor.

The water samples – those old jars of murky, brown water from the river – seemed the furthest things from their minds.

Willson knew it could work, but he didn't quite know how. He knew that children's learning didn't depend on how tightly controlled their curriculum program came to them. Learning out of a textbook or off a computer program worked for some students in school, but it barely tapped their interest or ingenuity, or the experiences and knowledge that they brought with them to school from home or the community. For some students, this type of rote learning would yield more advantages, goods if you will, like college admission and jobs awarded as a result of test performance. Otherwise, the knowledge students acquired in school added little value to their lives, none they could trace back to school learning in math or the language arts.

Adults had long ago decided that students' interests and lives could be ignored in school, that society had a use for them knowing certain things but not much else. Basic knowledge became the catchword in all educational circles, for the most part, killing off any movements that privileged the student and the experience of learning in the real world. And teachers had become untrustworthy, merely controllable facilitators for a knowledge base that had been fixed in efficient technology.

This didn't happen overnight, but it did happen rather quickly. Teachers, ultimately, lost any control over the decisions about what would be taught on a day-to-day basis. Innocently enough, it seemed, this came as a result of the development of early state and district-wide curriculum guides back in the 1990s that mandated that certain materials and lessons and content to be taught on a daily basis. Some teachers even welcomed the changes early-on, feeling like it took a huge time and effort burden off them to decide what to teach and to organize it effectively. They didn't feel particularly skilled with curriculum matters in the first place, so they typically viewed the changes as helps.

Then a major computer company with a national network and a popular founding inventor and CEO, Clyde Strongman, who had built his fortune and contacts through a long string of friendly government contacts and contracts, began a movement in the western states to standardize the entire elementary and secondary curricula and to load the grade-leveled curricula he had developed by so-called experts in all subjects into computer programs.

Strongman marketed whole systems of computers and programs that schools began to buy. Pretty soon, several states had adopted the "Strongman Learning Systems" and put them into classrooms, then into entire schools, then into entire school districts, then into entire states. Books became obsolete, and so did knowledge that lay outside the standard curriculum on the new computers, thereby challenging libraries and public schools as they were widely understood to stay relevant, a challenge they couldn't meet as a result of their antiquated technology and under-funding. The system became such a "natural" part of the school system that Strongman took his name off the computers and anything else that might normally need to be branded for marketing purposes. He held a monopoly on the product and he held the grip tightly. The systems just *were*. He made a fortune, many times over.

Testing companies tapped into the wave of reform, working with Strongman to create high stakes tests that soon governed the way citizens judged schools and districts and cities to live in. Teachers balked at first, especially when it became clear that they had not only lost the curriculum but also any say over how the curriculum would be taught. But teachers who resisted were dismissed or shouted down by those who thought they were standing in the way of legitimate reforms, the kinds that would really help schools. No matter how misinformed, these enforcers had power and the support of the state fully behind them.

Teachers maintained their status in society as purveyors of the new reforms, but they soon realized that they had basically become data entry specialists. The whole public education system as it had come to be known since the World War II era toppled in about five years time. It seemed as if there were no way things could swing back. Then Sam Sanders walked out on the test and Pete Willson taught *Huck Finn*, out of the real book and out of the blue, no less.

What people had mostly forgotten that became evident again in Downing when the students began reading books and connecting their ideas regarding texts and their experiences in the world – primarily through representational forms such as writing and art and music – was that students of all ages have experiences and a rich base of knowledge from their lives in communities with families and friends that they bring to school. If this wealth is tapped into, it can produce deep, rich learning and experiences for students, for the school, and for the community.

The trick, which Pete Willson had begun to understand very well after just a few short weeks of teaching again, was figuring out how to go about re-educating teachers and students to approach learning as an activity that is constructed in the complex interplay of relationships, communication, study, and experience. So the questions become:

How do you create value for searching, inquiring, and learning when there might not be any correct answers in sight and a long road toward mastery? How do you teach people to value the journey toward knowledge over the ending point or destination? How is a questioning, inquiry-oriented stance valuable as the primary mode for learning, and not just an exceptional side-show activity following more "basic" and "essential" studies in school? How can learning lead to social value and perhaps even social action on the part of students, who might discover through school and advanced learning how to live lives both emboldened and bolstered by their experiences with democracy and learning that are relevant, invigorating, and illuminating? How do you do complex activities with students anyway, especially if they don't seem to have the necessary 'basics' to start with?

All of these questions swirled in Willson's head, even as he taught, and even as he planned, and even as he mowed the lawn. He couldn't escape them; so he decided to view them as helps, and he used his constant preoccupation with the educational questions at hand to guide his practice. He let the questions and the ideas guide him as he worked with his new teammates, and as he talked with students. He worked hard to think of and act on this teaching as the work of helping students create knowledge. He tried less and less to view himself as a language arts specialist who imparted static knowledge to students to regurgitate back to him without using it in any meaningful way; instead, he thought of himself as an educated person who was learning right along with his students, sometimes on material that he himself felt to be relatively unfamiliar to him. Sometimes the students themselves became the experts, and taught him a thing or two. He knew when this happens that things are going right, not wrong.

Early the next morning, Willson met with the team. They had the whole first period of the day, almost 90 minutes, to plan together. They shared their progress with the students and with the curriculum taking shape in the classrooms as they taught. Jerry and Mary had been clearly moved by their classroom experiences with students and their planning activities together over the past few days. They each had received a phone call from Ms. Belders at the public library the night before. They had quite a story to tell.

55 – LIKE DOMINOS TUMBLING

Jerry said, "Mary called me on the phone and told me that she had gotten a call from Ms. Belders about 4 pm. I said, 'Me, too.' Then I asked her, 'What did Belders say?' Mary gives me basically the same story that Ms. Belders gave me. She says, 'I received this box of material from Stevens' estate with a letter. Sam has looked at it with me, and we can't really figure it out. Would you like to come down and glance at it and tell me if you think there is anything here that you might want to use for class? I heard that you were doing a water study with your classes and thought this might help.'"

Jerry and Mary looked at each other, excited about what had happened, and what might possibly lie ahead.

Pete smiled. He interpreted Bert's discomforting grimace and asked, "What's wrong Bert?"

"Nobody called me. What am I? Chopped liver?"

They all laughed roundly, and settled in for the story.

Mary continued, "It's like this mystery box at the library so we just had to go. I called Jerry and we decided to meet Belders at the library at 8 pm. As a teacher before, I never did anything like this and didn't really care to do so, after all everything was already decided for me in terms of what was important to know and important to teach. But now I feel like learning, and getting involved. I'm just energized by this whole thing, and at the same time I really can't put my finger on it or tell you what it is or why I feel differently now. Anyway, we met at the library, and looked through this box of papers and this letter that Stevens wrote to Belders. It was fascinating, really, like trying to crack a code. This box was just full of files with papers that had what looked like conversations between at least two people over some chemistry questions or problems. We couldn't figure it out on the spot, so we brought copies of the pages we think are most relevant, as well as a copy of the letter from Stevens. We thought maybe if we could get a general sense of their meaning that we could use the documents in class as primary sources. Here, Pete, the copy of the letter is for you, really."

"Thanks," replied Pete, taking the letter from Mary. "How do you think this all ties into our curriculum?"

Jerry offered, "I think that something happened years ago between Stevens and Sanders and they had a discussion about the chemistry of some process or other happening down at the plant. I know Sanders was smart, but I had no idea that he and Stevens both knew chemistry so well, or so it seems. When I looked at the papers I recognized quite a few references to H_2O, or water, of course. Something must have been happening at the plant that required a lot of extra water or threatened the water supply or something. We all know what the plant did to pollute our water supply years ago, and how we had to develop 'space-age' filters to get the impurities out of it for consumption. Thank goodness for Dr. Percy and his work for the city, or we all would have been poisoned long ago."

They nodded in agreement, and Jerry continued, "Perhaps all of this is related to Sanders' death, too. We all know about the controversy at the plant between Sanders and Stevens over putting in that reading library for workers. Why such animosity between them? Why would Stevens call Sanders 'partner' in the letter? How did Sanders die and why? I mean, all of this is salient. What can we bring up with the students? How should we approach this with them?"

Bert said, "This is all making perfect sense to me now."

Every head turned toward Bert, and they looked at him astonished.

He went on, "Look, don't act so surprised, you might hurt my feelings. I may have been a certain type of teacher for long time, but I'm no idiot. Here's how I see it. Let's have the students examine these primary documents in language arts class. There are lots of lessons to be learned by doing that, like determining authenticity of text, interpreting the text, clarifying genre, etc. and by having students produce their own poetry or drama related to the themes that Willson has been driving home such as caring for the environment and the entire planet."

Bert had to stop for a moment; his colleagues were all taking notes.

"At the same time, let's continue the water supply study by narrowing it down according to the meaning that the students can make from these documents and their content. Maybe in their explorations and experiments we'll discover what Stevens meant. Let's encourage Mary to get the students involved in an interview study with residents who may have worked in the plant back in '09 and who might remember this whole controversy. And last, I'll help students run the statistics and equations on the data they gather from the water study. I know that many of the things we have been working on will apply to their experiments. The connecting, culminating project will be a small group report, say of four persons on a team, on the topic 'The relationship of home water supply to quality of life.' What do you say?"

Stunned, Mary Baldwin kept scribing, then put her pen down, threw up her hands and said, "By golly, 'The Eagle Has Landed!' Are you kidding me? This is truly a landmark event, my friends. Not only does he get it, but Bert has been holding back on us. Let's get this thing going. We have so much work to do."

Bert blushed a little, then said, "Come on, let's get started."

With that speech, and after a few pats on the back around the table, the teachers began planning their approach and its significant details in the curriculum for the next two weeks. Never before had there been so much energy and passion around their table. It was the first of many more such times to come.

When Sam saw Maggie he smiled broadly, from ear to ear. She had to have seen it coming. He pulled a muddy jar out of his pocket and handed it to her when she sat down at her desk, right at the sounding of second bell.

"You missing something?" he asked.

"Where did you find it? I've been looking all over. I knew I had one more of those jars," she responded.

"Back seat of my car," he grinned.

"Come on, we didn't spend any time *there* last night. It must have rolled out of my pocket or something," she teased back.

"Must have, I guess," he smiled, too.

"Okay, class, let's get down to it now," called Jerry Strigent. "We're going on our data field trip today. We have 90 minutes, so we have plenty of time to get there and back and for your teams to get plenty of samples. Here are a few tips for taking and storing your samples."

Mr. Strigent demonstrated proper collection and storage techniques for taking samples at the lake and then kicked the discussion back to students.

"What questions do you have before we go?"

Maggie spoke up.

"I just wanted to give you a couple of jars of advanced samples that we collected last night, Mr. Strigent. We got a few jars at the river and used a few techniques from this book we got from Ms. Belders to do some early analysis. According to our findings, these samples have an unusually high quantity of 4 different things: hydrogen, oxygen, beron, and nitrogen, plus one we can't identify." The class turned around and just looked at Maggie, nearly stunned silent. Initiative held a rather novel place in the being and acting of Downing adolescents. They could take initiative…they just hadn't seen it modeled much before this.

Sam followed up, "We don't know much about this element beron and we must identify this other element. We need to learn more about it and try to figure out why there seems to be so much of it in our water. Why is it there? Is it hurting us?"

Mr. Strigent, duly impressed, responded, "Terrific, you two. What a tremendous start of baseline data. Class, we'll use Maggie and Sam's findings as springboards for judging our first collective samples as a class, okay? And, at some point this week, we'll need to replicate the experiments they performed in order to test their conclusions. A small team of volunteers can do that for us right here in our lab. Marvelous. Any other questions?"

Assuming no one else had anything that could match their display and needing to get the students out of the class, Strigent adjourned the class to the bus and they rode together to the lake site.

Once there, students began to collect samples in teams. Across the 15 teams, the class generated 60 new water samples. The team members carefully documented the source and location of each sample from various locations around the lake. They marked the jars and placed them in a large container. They completed the task fairly quickly, in about 30 minutes. It would have taken a team of merely 3 or 4 people several hours to collect and document that many samples. Mr. Strigent planned on bringing several more groups out to the lake that day. He thought he'd get at least 100 different samples from that body of water. This would give a thorough-going mass of material for each class to analyze.

Once back in the classroom, Mr. Strigent asked the class, "What was that like? Did you feel like scientists?"

Marjorie answered, "I thought it was kind of boring until we started seeing different colorations in the water from different parts of the lake. I didn't anticipate that, or that you could even get a visual on the color differences. I thought most of the things we found out about the water would be microscopic and not even visible to the naked eye."

Clem's hand shot up and he responded, "Well, I anticipate that the real show will come when we start performing experiments on different samples. I'm interested if we'll see beron in the water like Sam and Maggie found in the river's supply and if we'll be figuring out what that means if we do."

Sarah jumped in, "Yeah, see, I'm just wandering," she puzzled out loud, "how is it that we will choose what things we want to do with the water? I mean, we don't know much about chemistry and we've never even used microscopes or mixed chemicals together? Where do we even start?"

Before Strigent had a chance to respond, Maggie did.

"I felt the same way, Sarah. But Sam and I started reading this book from like 1978 by Lisa Minzer called *Amateur Chemists at Work in the Community* and it was really clear in terms of charting stages in the scientific process for working on science issues in the community that might be related to social issues surrounding pollution and the like," she took a big breath, that was a long sentence. The class giggled with her. She continued without missing more than this one beat, as serious she could be and surrounded by students just as serious as they could be about doing something meaningful with the materials they had to work with.

"Apparently, these social and political activists from late in the last century got interested in teaching students how to track down sources of water pollution in their communities. With the advent of the curriculum on computers and our boring school existences as we used to know them, this type of self-directed and socially useful learning approach went out of style. In some cases, students' findings caused such a stir that companies shut down and lawyers had big paydays. Some, no doubt, believe that these curricular 'successes' may have led to the downfall of experience-based learning. Powerful people no doubt questioned how this type of powerful learning did anything but hurt corporations and the powers that be."

If Mr. Strigent felt somewhat stunned by the eloquence and the depth of thought exhibited so far by his students, then Rex Houndson brought him back to earth.

"You know, Mr. Strigent, this is all a bunch of hogwash. With all due respect, we don't have any more business being out on the loose acting like scientists as we would acting like police at a crime scene or fire fighters at a fire. That takes skill and know-how. This is stupid. We don't even know what we're doing, and we're just wasting time collecting stupid samples and then doing some lame experiments on them. I don't have even the remotest interest in science or in this project. I went along today, but it's going to get harder for me every day to stay involved. My dad owns a sandwich shop. I don't want people poking around my garbage and finding out there's a bunch of X in the bread and then running my dad out of business. How does that get us anywhere? How does this prepare me to run that shop or to keep people working for me later?"

Strigent, not used to responding much to students' remarks on either a positive or negative note because no one ever responded and he rarely spoke to students in class for years at a time, thought carefully before rebutting. There was a long silence, the students waited for him.

Then he said, "Rex, I'm sorry to hear that. For so long I just flipped on computers in this job. I've learned more useful knowledge about the world and about myself in the last couple of weeks than I learned in the past 20 years I've spent in school as a teacher and as a student, all together. Trust me, this might seem lame at times, but it's the real thing. I'll do my best to take you somewhere meaningful. At the end, let me know if you are still floundering. Okay? And, last, if your dad was hurting people at his shop, either feeding us something or throwing out something that poisoned us, we need to know that. It's not criminal to expose wrongdoing; but it's wrong to do nothing out of ignorance, or out of pure self-interest, covering things up while folks get richer or stay oblivious and get hurt or hurt others as a result."

"Rock on, Mr. S.!" shouted Beverly in the front row. She continued, "My parents are older than most of all of my friends' parents and that makes my grandparents products of the sixties. You all know my parents adopted me later in life. They actually remember the 1960s because they were alive then. We haven't learned much about it because the curriculum we used to have barely paid any attention to it," she looked at Rex during this part of her response, then she turned back to addressing Mr. Strigent.

She continued, "The word I remember most associated with that period was 'abberation.' That's what our former curriculum used to say about it. My parents say the 60s are more than that, *if that*, and that for a while during that period people felt as if they had some say over how the world and government acted. Maybe we were more American in conflict than we ever have been as passive consumers since. They get excited thinking that we might get some of that back in our schools. They're tired of garbage being dumped in everybody's backyard and no one doing anything about it. They're tired of garbage being dumped in our schools through the curriculum and no one doing anything about it. Sam started this, let's see what happens. Let's do something about all the garbage out there."

The bell rang during her last sentence, and the class members rustled their books and papers and computers together and hustled out into the hallway to talk and chat and get ready for social studies with Ms. Baldwin. There, in Baldwin's class, the 1960s and their spirited interest in activism would certainly come alive. As if it hadn't already.

58 – GETTING DOWN TO IT

Ms. Baldwin had spread old newspapers out all over the classroom. When Sam and Maggie and their friends walked in they thought they might be getting to do an art project of some sort or other, like children used to do in school on a regular basis. Maybe the papers were meant to protect the floors from errant paint or paste spills. They soon learned otherwise, but weren't disappointed.

They sat at their desks and started to examine the yellowing newspapers. Ms. Baldwin stood by the doorway watching them.

Ms. Baldwin asked, after a few minutes of busy buzz and activity in the classroom: "Class, what can you tell me about these newspapers? Describe them."

"The year," offered Lizzie Pelton.

"What about the year?" Ms. Baldwin seized.

"This one is dated 2009, and so are all the others. They actually come from one part of the year, the spring, I think," now Lizzie wandered from desk to desk and table to table talking out loud to Ms. Baldwin and the class as she examined the artifacts.

"And now that you mention it," no one actually had mentioned anything of the sort, "the one thing they have in common is front page news on the plant and the controversy surrounding the Environmental Patents Group (EPG) and its involvement in the plant's pollution history. This article is headlined, 'Make way for EPG: Plant shut down again.' There must have been some serious issues out there during this period. I wonder what all was going on?"

Lizzie sat down and began reading the article. She got lost in it.

Others floated around looking at the articles. Some started taking notes as they moved. Others stayed put and read whole articles all the way through.

After about 30 minutes, Ms. Baldwin called for their attention, pulled them together, and began asking questions.

"Class, let's work on a few things together for a couple of minutes. First, tell me if these primary source documents are actually from the same general period."

Martin Boardman answered, "Yes, Ms. Baldwin, my group found that all of the articles come from the Spring of 2009. What is interesting is how much attention got paid to the issues surrounding Stevens' development of the 'water making process.' It really is fascinating that this technology was developed right here in Downing by one of our own citizens. Our local papers paid attention to it, focusing mainly on Stevens' achievements."

Michelle Patterson piped up, "And something else, later that spring, made this very interesting. It became known to everyone during the application for an environmental patent from the EPG that the element berol had been detected in the process. It somehow got produced when Stevens combined the elements necessary for making water together. This byproduct is supposed to be harmless, but the EPG put a limit on how much of it could be produced in a year and how it had to be safely disposed of."

"And also," Patrick Knight's hand shot up and his mouth opened at the same time, "it became clear that a huge amount of water would be necessary for the cooling process to work. Somehow I think this must be tied to the pollution problems that we had years ago that Dr. Percy helped solve. But we don't have enough information. It is remarkable, though, that right here in Downing someone invented a process for making water that had only been dreamed of by scientists for generations."

Ms. Baldwin jumped in, "Excellent start. You are right, Patrick, we don't have enough information." Ms. Baldwin walked to the storage closet, and pulled out a box of papers, filled mostly with file folders and a few stray papers, the old lined kind that people used to write on in school.

"Rex Houndson, your team will begin the process of trying to understand the significance of these papers. They mostly have science content," the papers were copies of the ones that Belders had received from Stevens just the day before. "But we need to know how they are connected to the water plant and this story. There is some social significance to all of these events that I'm afraid still have some bearing on today. Most of the teachers on our team think that they are somehow connected, but we don't know how. Your team is charged with taking a first look at the documents and telling the class what it is you think they mean, at least give us a few ideas. I'm giving it to your team and not the whole class. It's too complicated, and too many people working on it would confuse things. Here…" and with that she plopped the huge box down on his team's table.

Rex simply rolled his eyes. He hadn't been buying this so far, and had been paying little attention anyway. Ms. Baldwin's seeming vote of confidence, or bestowal of responsibility, felt too easy to read.

"Yeah, right, Ms. Baldwin, give the most important job to the rabble-rouser. You think you can convert me? Don't be too sure," Rex said matter-of-factly and with defiance, as he leaned his chair on its two back legs and moved his toothpick from side to side in his mouth, acting like he just didn't care. Truth be told, he didn't.

"I'm not sure, Rex, about your ability to do this, either, in terms of your will. Intelligence? Talent, intellect, raw ability to do the work? No problems. But, otherwise, in fact, I'm very skeptical based on what you have shown me so far. But I don't want to discount the other three members of your team and their interest and curiosity. We'll see."

"Yeah, we'll see," Rex put the front legs of his chair back down and picked up his bag and walked out. Ms. Baldwin let him go.

"He'll be back, class. He'll be back…Okay, now where were we? Right. Your assignment is to write a short synopsis of the content of the article in the newspaper at your desk. Jesse and Willis' teams will compile the synopses and look for patterns, common threads."

59 – FRIED CHICKEN DINNER, AGAIN

It had become rather common for Mrs. Sanders to invite Mr. Willson for dinner. She always made fried chicken for him. Sam didn't mind, he rather looked forward to the meals, and especially to the banter around the table. He almost always learned something from them that he didn't know yet.

Tonight Pete arrived at around 6 pm, a little later than usual. Sam had no plans to see Maggie – she had to eat out with her family – and he had all of his homework finished, so he played ball in the drive until Willson showed up in his truck. Willson had the original box of papers with him.

"Hey, what's with the papers? I can't seem to get away from those things," called Sam. For sure, they had traveled well over the last few days.

"Well, son, you know," Willson offered as he approached, "I thought your mom should see these. They were your dad's notes after all, and she should know about them. People all over town are looking at them."

"Yeah, well, she's got chicken on and we're due inside. Let's go."

Pete followed Willson inside and Willson plopped the papers down on the table.

Betsy turned around, so glad to see them. But then her smile turned sour when she saw the box. She couldn't believe her eyes. The distinctive files, the tabs that read "Chemistry: Sanders." It all came rushing back to her; she dropped her tongs and fainted, straight to the floor. Chicken grease splattered all over with the pan left uncovered and its tender laid out flat on the floor.

"Betsy, Betsy," Pete pleaded with her as he held her hands and gently slapped her cheeks trying to make her come to. Sam turned off the stove and got some water for her.

"Mom? What is it? What's wrong? Oh, good gosh, come on, come on, Mom?" Sam panicked as he shook her shoulders, leaning down on the floor with Willson now.

Betsy's eyes rolled a bit as she came out of it and she put her hand over her brow, beat, lying there rather helplessly on the cold linoleum. Sweat poured from her forehead. They sat her up in a chair at the table and gave her some water. She drank from the glass, shaky-like, several drops spilling down her neck, which Willson gently dried with a kitchen towel. Grease still spattered into the air and fell on the floor, hot. But she just stared at the file box on the table, mute, nearly catatonic.

After a few moments more, she asked in a whisper, "Where did you get those files?"

Willson responded, "Honey, Belders got them from Stevens with this note."

He showed her the note. He read it carefully to her, out loud.

She looked at each of them, one at a time, and then put her head down into her hands and knees.

"I haven't seen those files for 15 years. It's a part of our past that I didn't want to come out. When I started to write back and forth with Stevens, Paul supported me but didn't feel all that comfortable with it, seeing as he had to deliver all of the files back and forth," her voice trailed off and she took another sip of water.

Sam, astonished, asked his mother for clarification. He looked at Willson, searchingly, thinking he might have something to add as well, but Willson simply shrugged. He didn't know anything about this. "Mom, what do you mean when you say *you* started to write back and forth with Stevens?"

"Well, it doesn't have to be a secret anymore," she said spiritedly, her voice and color coming back. "I'm tired of secrets," they lifted her carefully into a kitchen chair. "I spoke with Stevens at a holiday party years ago regarding his project for combining elements to make water. He was talking about combining liquid hydrogen and oxygen to make water. I thought it was outlandish, considering how chemists and nuclear scientists had been working on it for years and had made so little progress. I actually laughed it off. But I loved chemistry in high school, I actually took a summer course on it at the college between junior and senior year. He could tell I knew some things, and he started sending me these formulas and Paul would bring them home. Sometimes we worked on the formulas together, sometimes Paul wrote my notes for me as I talked them out. I started writing back to Stevens, showing where I thought he might be in error or outlining what he should be thinking about instead. I never charged him for it, I just enjoyed chemistry."

She paused briefly, now addressing Sam directly. "I stayed home with you, Sam, and at odd hours when you were napping I just sat down and wrote, playing around with formulas, brainstorming sort of. Sometimes Ms. Belders would help me find the right book to look something up. Paul dutifully carried the files back and forth. He was so supportive after awhile. Ultimately, he didn't care in the least that I had this outside interest. He thought it was great."

Sam and Pete couldn't believe their ears; they didn't find it odd that Betsy knew the chemistry, but she never let on that it interested her in any other part of her life before or since. She never mentioned this relationship with Stevens when Paul died or after Stevens shot at them. Pete couldn't even remember science being something that interested Betsy when she was in school. At root, they just didn't know if they could take any more surprises.

After awhile, they finished cooking up the chicken and ate it up. Betsy's appetite came back, none of them could resist the chicken. After clearing the table, they dug into the files again. Betsy held a cold compress on her forehead while they worked.

Betsy explained some of the finer points of the papers as she understood them from years past. She told her version of events:

"Look, here's the last page we sent back and forth. I confirm that the process Stevens proposed for making water would work with the correct amount of cooling force simultaneously combined at the point of combustion. He agrees here...see? We both understood this strange phenomenon with the berol production. That would be a problem, but not something that couldn't be overcome."

She glanced through several more files. She came upon a yellow folder, with only one sheet of paper in it and written in a hand that looked like Paul's. On the bottom of the paper were printed the word 'aluminum' and then a date 'March 15, 2024' then the periodic table abbreviation for it, 'al.' It also had the word 'Me' and the symbol '$' next to it. Very strange.

Betsy puzzled, "I've never seen this piece of paper before and I have no idea what it means. Paul must have written it. But what does aluminum have to do with anything substantive? And why did this get added so late? All of my writing with Stevens took place years before? We all found out later that aluminum piping couldn't carry the water to the cooling device because it is toxic, thanks to Dr. Percy. The EPG made us take out huge sections of it that cost Stevens millions and the aluminum manufacturer even more. So this doesn't make any sense. Aluminum? Aluminum? It can't be possible that Paul knew anything more than we know now. No, it can't be."

"No, it can't be, dear. It wasn't his fault that the piping had too high a concentration of aluminum. Everyone knew that too much is really bad. It wasn't his fault that the piping proved to be faulty, just because he put it in. He couldn't have known."

"Maybe," Betsy half-heartedly agreed, "but why would Paul have written this such a short time ago if he didn't know something else? What could it have been? And why wouldn't he have told anyone? And could it have been the thing that came between Stevens and Paul? I feel like we are really close to something, but that it is still buried somehow. My fear is that it is probably buried with him, along with the reason why he died. He loved me, he did, and he wouldn't leave us on purpose..." She broke down now, sobbing quietly while Pete and Sam comforted her. This was a lot to take in, even given that Paul had been gone for a while and Pete had come along. So much still didn't make sense.

They quickly tired after that, and Pete said goodnight. Sam put his mom to bed, and stayed up with the papers and pondered. "Aluminum? Money? Me?" Sam reviewed in his own mind what everyone else in town knew, and learned in the community as a result of living there.

Everyone knew that Dr. Percy had discovered the large amount of aluminum in the water five years ago and had installed filtering devices to purify the natural and the man-made water supplies. These filters took care of the berol problem, which hadn't come back in any significant amounts. Many believed that the residue from the original aluminum piping caused the problem, including about 4 cases of tumor-like masses that killed the infected people almost instantly, usually in less than a month. It had been a mystery until Percy tested the pipes and found the large concentrations of aluminum. This disaster had proven to be a heavy burden on Stevens' company and on Paul; but the community had put this honest mistake behind and so had Paul, or so all had thought.

It wasn't really anyone's fault, except for maybe the manufacturer of the aluminum; and this group had handled much of the financial burden caused by the plague that ensued. The aluminum manufacturer paid for damages to families, as well as for the costs of re-rigging the water plant with new piping, and then for the work done by Percy to battle the aluminum in the water supply with his special filters. They even helped pay for lost revenue that resulted from panic about the safety of the water produced at the plant (a judge had ordered it). The aluminum manufacturer, as a result of these costs, went bankrupt, exhausting its insurance and so damaging its reputation that no one would buy its aluminum, even at rock-bottom prices. The manufacturer went completely out of business and its CEOs wound up penniless, disgraced. But Stevens managed to stay in business, just barely. The plant had risen from the ashes to become the richest (and for awhile the only) producer of "man-made water" in the world.

In the end, no one blamed Paul. No one ever brought it up. It had become moot. Paul's crew had installed the piping, but no one assigned blame to him or Stevens. After about three years, Percy determined that his very expensive filters had done the trick. The filters were removed and things had gotten back to normal in Downing since all the bad piping had been removed. But what did this memo mean? And why had Stevens brought it up? It obviously held the key to some mystery, or would prove to be the more figurative smoking gun. But for what?

61 – BIG TEACH

Many years earlier, Dr. Dormont worked in a high school in San Antonio, Texas, where students themselves took responsibility for teaching large group gatherings of their own classmates on the same grade level. They called the sessions a "Big Teach," during which students would teach a lesson or explore a topic in the big group. The teachers helped, but they left most of the decisions to the students. Usually, all of the students had been working on a similar project or theme or concept; the Big Teach helped to check progress, congeal ideas and learning, and surface possibilities for next steps. Dr. Dormont suggested the format to Willson when he reported to her what had been found out during the past couple of days regarding the ninth grade class' first major project, built around themes in environmental science. After several days of planning, the school scheduled the Big Teach for second period the next day.

When everyone had assembled, Student Facilitator Phil Jamison asked Sam Sanders to come up front to the podium to give a short presentation highlighting the developments to date. Sam gave a thorough description of the class' work on the water sample collections, even incorporating a poem from Willson's class in his analysis of the activity; he explained how groups had been working on the Stevens/Sanders papers and some of the strange developments there, especially the finding of the memo more recently dated in his father's hand to Stevens with those simple words and symbols "aluminum" and "al" noted, as well as the word "Me" and the symbol "$." This bit of information set off a stir at Rex Houndson's table. His team members began to converse excitedly; two of them left the room almost immediately.

Several other members of the class came up to the podium after Sam and reported on their activities to date. Phil Jamison acted as the facilitator, finally calling for students to offer up summary statements about what they thought had been achieved and learned to date. The teachers stood along the wall, taking notes and listening intently, not wanting to miss anything and not interrupting.

At the end of the last speaker's time, Rex Houndson's table erupted again once his two teammates came back. They handed Rex a piece of paper and urged him to go up to the front. Reluctantly, Rex made his way to the front of the room and the podium. Phil Jamison, the student facilitator, asked Rex, "Would you like to come up here, Rex? It looks like you have something to report."

Rex walked slowly to the podium, still examining the writing on the paper. He spoke eloquently, though not always glowingly about the project and his team's work to date:

"Well, most of you know how stupid I think all this is. I don't know that we are really learning anything. My group got stuck looking at all those documents in the box. Well, we didn't find anything in there. We didn't find that memo Sanders is talking about that he supposedly found last night at his house. But that's pretty cool, regardless, because it made me realize that when my group was running tests for trace elements on our water samples the other day that we never tested for aluminum. We were just messing around testing for toxins and such, but not aluminum. Given that Doc Percy said it was okay a few years back to take out the filter system, we didn't even think of testing for aluminum. We found trace elements of other chemicals, minerals, elements all at safe levels in the water, including berol. But my team associates just ran a simple test for aluminum that they found in the book that Sam brought to school and that we have been using as a guide for our sampling techniques on the water. You won't believe this, but we found astonishingly high levels of aluminum in our samples. We don't know if these are whacky samples, if someone is playing games with us, or what. We just know you won't believe the high levels of aluminum. Our calculations reveal them to be at exceptionally high toxic levels. That's all I've got."

Rex walked back to his seat, still stunned at the possible meaning of their discovery. Deep down, he realized that it might not be possible to trace the logical, reasonable steps in the learning that had just taken place, but he knew perhaps that his group had saved many residents of Downing from certain doom.

Friends and teachers patted him on the back all the way back to his seat despite the sobering possibilities of the news.

Willson went to the podium.

"Class, this much is clear. We owe a debt of gratitude to Rex's team and to all of you who have been working hard to try to figure out the complex problems and puzzles you have been presented with. I want to make an assignment for the rest of the day, even though I haven't discussed this with my colleagues. We've gotten to know each other and how we think so well that I think they'll agree, and if they don't they'll speak up in this space. We need to run tests for aluminum content on all of the samples we have collected. Please take every precaution to systematize your procedures, and carefully and accurately enter your results. I'm asking Mr. Convoyan to assist the entire class in the statistical analysis of the results. I'm calling in the health department right now so that they can take a more formal role from here on out, including running their own official tests and issuing public warnings. That's really their job and they are well-trained to do it. If we know anything about aluminum poisoning it's that it doesn't wait around for people to get ready for it. Everyone will get a tutorial from Houndson's group in the main lab on how to run the test and enter the results, and then we'll split into teams. Let's go. Houndson, you lead the way. I want the social action team and the safety team to report up here to the teachers to discuss how to work with Missy Tallons to get a public statement out from the school. We should do that as quickly as possible. That's Emerson, Lake, and Palmer's groups. Let's go."

No one said anything. They just moved. The students got up and moved directly to their classrooms. Dr. Dormont already had her phone out calling the health department and trying to get hold of Dr. Percy.

Pete and the teachers met briefly before adjourning with the students to their lab stations. They spent the rest of the day and long after school running samples. They compared their results to those generated quickly by the health department scientists sent out to the school immediately to work with the same samples. Simultaneously, a collection team gathered more samples from area water sources and brought them to the school to be tested. The sets of figures yielded a remarkable consistency. The levels of toxicity findings came within one hundredths of each other. The fact of the matter was that water poisoned by aluminum threatened Downing residents again. Word spread quickly in the community, and residents took every precaution not to consume the water. The press had a field day with the news, especially with the fact that this "new" school program had revealed the danger as a result of student activity.

Rex Houndson, for sure, knew one thing more that afternoon than he knew that morning: the answer to the mystery was in that box, and maybe already revealed in some form. He just knew it.

The health department seized all of the files in Stevens' box when they came that afternoon. The school had already made copies of the files, and Houndson's group kept the master copy made from the documents. They pored over the documents one by one, analyzing them, cataloguing qualities of each one looking for some sort of pattern or key locked in the document and unavailable to the layperson's eye.

This went on for several weeks at school. Members of the group took the documents home with them. So did other groups, but none with the same intensity of Houndson's group and of Houndson himself. Rex's group studied every angle it could think of, drawing on language arts and science and music and social studies and art and math, every thing they had learned to date, and pursuing every lead that the documents gave them. So far, they had come up empty, or so it seemed. But Rex had a determination fueled by that one insight to test for aluminum that came to him at the Big Teach. That insight acted like a constant, addictive catalyst to keep him inquiring, learning. Houndson had an idea now that he couldn't shake; his pursuit of knowledge might actually mean something to society beyond his doing well on the tests, or getting into a good college, or landing a good job. He had never thought about the purpose of education this way before. He hated the idea of Baldwin's being right, but he knew now that she was. Perhaps education could reflect life itself and lead to social goods that benefited all, not just the elite few who could participate in the individual goods that accrue to the traditionally educated high achievers like he had earlier been destined to become.

On a crisp fall Monday morning, Dr. Dormont appeared at the Ms. Baldwin's door. She called Rex over and handed him a telegram. Telegrams, once common – then only used occasionally in the era of email and high-speed communication – only rarely appeared in special life circumstances during the 2020s. Dr. Dormont had not opened it, although she could have. It was addressed to "Rex Houndson, in care of Dr. Cynthia Dormont." The return address was the state's Supreme Court, Richway. She handed it to Rex and said, "Go ahead, open it. It's addressed to you."

Rex stood there dumbfounded. He clumsily tore open the envelope and pulled out the card from inside. He read it out loud to the class, at Dormont's prompting, the words and format stultifying at first, but quaintly formal and official in the end, and highly effective:

Dear Mr Houndson stop I understand that you and your classmates at Downing High School found that the residents of Downing once again were being poisoned by aluminum stop Congratulations on your finding and keep up the good work stop Your work no doubt has made a significant contribution to the public good and health of our citizens stop I look forward to meeting you when you present your inquiries and learnings to the high court this spring stop See you in March stop Chief Justice Haskins stop

None of them could imagine a scenario in which Rex Houndson would tear up. But he couldn't make it through the last few lines of the telegram. He froze up, caught in the emotion of having done something worthwhile and getting caught doing it. He felt strangely proud and unworthy all at the same time. He made a vow to the class:

"No matter what, we need to find out where this poison is coming from."

Rex sat back down and the class got back to work. When all was said and done, it proved to be one of the team's most productive days.

63 – KEEPING TRACK OF
TEACHING AND LEARNING

All of the teachers at the high school knew that a huge challenge of the new curriculum would be keeping track of it. In order to cover as many bases as possible, the students and teachers developed together a system for keeping running records of activities and findings. Each activity included a rationale for it, a sentence or two on connections to other learning activities or ideas, a description of what happened, and a speculation on the results. If student work had been produced during the activity, students chose several of the best products and included them in the report. Students entered these reports as records into a database for each school date of the year.

Teddy Hersh held students and teachers accountable; she took on the responsibility of monitoring the gathering of the data. Jerry Strigent helped the teams develop a complex computer program that connected lessons and activities together by keywords. This appeared rather difficult to some at first, but once students and teachers got into the routine of completing their reports they could see how important it was for the program. Also, it offered another opportunity in school to practice skills and concepts in language arts and the arts, since the school purposefully used a wide range of representational formats to show learning including mathematics, writing, music, art, etc.

After 12 weeks, Teddy ran a report showing the connections between the curriculum being developed by students and teachers at the school and the traditional curriculum being taught through the computer systems.

The Downing curriculum had covered 93% of the content required by the standardized curriculum. That meant that through Downing's emergent curriculum students had the opportunity to learn more than 9/10s of what more traditionally educated students had been learning through their computer-based curricula. Much more important, the Downing curriculum documented the offering of an extra 1,288 learning opportunities of facts, ideas, or concepts through group and independent inquiries to the Downing student than the state's typical school experience to that point. So for instance, down the road in Fletcher's Schools, students did not have the opportunity to learn upwards of a 1000 things that Downing's students had learned with its innovative curriculum, even in this short amount of time.

Everyone knew how important it would be to show people that students at Downing didn't experience a less rigorous curriculum but that they would learn just as much and no doubt more as a result of their participation in the emerging program.

The teachers and students sailed on through the school year together addressing topics and projects such as human rights, freedom, wars and disease, comparative economics, etc. The projects associated with these bigger topics always hit close to home. The world came to Downing during this school year. The school had no shortage of luminaries interested in supporting or debunking the school's "new" approaches to teaching and learning and many of them wrote to the school or came to the school to speak or to participate in learning for a day. The school took on all comers. It practiced open and engaging inquiry with everyone it came in contact with.

Of course, in the back of everyone's minds there remained the specter of the Stevens/Sanders case. The aluminum problem got solved quickly when Dr. Percy volunteered to put the aluminum filters back into the water system. As far as anyone knew, no one had gotten sick from drinking the water. There remained no doubt that some major problem continued to taint the water system, and Houndson's group continued with the project of trying to find out what it was that caused the tainting or kept serving as the source of the tainting long after the unit had been completed in the school and other projects and learning opportunities had come along.

Rex and his group kept coming back to that late document Paul Sanders had penned quickly to Stevens so late in his life, just days, actually, before he had been killed in the car accident. The group believed there was more than a clue in that memo, but a message. Perhaps it was more than a warning about the possible existence of aluminum remaining the water supply. The text, scrawled at the bottom of some very complex chemistry formulas at the top, read, "Aluminum   al   me $"

64 – PUTTING TWO AND TWO TOGETHER

For the longest time, Rex and his group hadn't thought much more about the symbols and words on Sanders final note past the possibility of the note being a warning about aluminum contamination. They felt suspicious about the 'me' and '$' markings, but didn't really quite know how to go about interrogating them. The group had so little to go on especially since Paul Sanders was dead, and since Betsy had written most of the memos, and didn't recall seeing and certainly hadn't written this one.

But one day over coffee with his inquiry group in the cafeteria, Rex started to wonder out loud. His line of thought had been spurred by a *Record Eagle* article by Missy Tallons written way back in '09 about the controversy over Paul Sanders' interest in starting a reading group for workers at the plant and how Stevens had crushed it, saying that this sort of activity decreased productivity and didn't have to do with workers' training, merely pleasure which they could get at home or at the library, but not at work.

"Guys, you know, I wonder…what did Paul Sanders mean by these symbols? They have to fit somewhere. These folks didn't just write whimsical notes back and forth for fun. They always meant something; they were always purposeful. What we know for sure – and I realize that we have been over this a million times, but we have to do it one more time, indulge me, okay – is that Sanders understood intimately and deeply after he installed the aluminum piping that it all needed to come out. Years later, aluminum reappears in the water supply after the filters had been turned off for several years, with us thinking that the contamination threat had been eliminated and all…"

His voice didn't trail but built with energy, his mind and body twitching now, with the excitement that more layers of the possible story would fit into place – as he talked it through – in ways they hadn't up to that point.

"…But then after millions of dollars of costs associated with removing the contaminating piping, and after Stevens nearly loses the whole operation, Sanders finds out or reveals that there remains a source of contamination. Just think of it, the power that Sanders would have over Stevens with this information. Do you think it is possible that Sanders either made sure that part of the piping remained in place, to slowly contaminate the water supply and to hold as a sort of bargaining chip over Stevens, or that he had made a mistake of not getting it all out and then later realized what it would cost Stevens to go back in and replace this essential infrastructure? Or do you think they both knew, and agreed to keep quiet, perhaps with Stevens even paying Sanders off to keep mum? Or do you think that they both knew they had gotten most of it out of the system but couldn't afford to get it all and with the filters in place protecting the public anyway felt little need to take the last step? And what about this curious stand-off over the library at the plant? I mean, how strange is that? What would a millionaire many times over like Stevens care about his workers learning to read better unless Sanders might use it as an opportunity to reveal his secret?"

Rex paused for a moment, completely worked up, and shouted, "That's got to be it! And yet, I don't know anything except one thing for sure...I think there's only one way to find out what really happened. We have to talk to Stevens and ask him these questions, which isn't going to be easy. Certainly, Paul Sanders knew something about the aluminum poisoning coming back and he knew that he was involved and that money was at stake. How it all fits together, we can only speculate. Stevens holds the secret. We have to talk with Stevens. Let's go."

They all got up from the table at the same time and found Willson in his classroom reading from student journals and preparing for the next day's class.

65 – GETTING CLOSER TO THE TRUTH

Of course, Willson loved Houndson's spunk. Pete had seen so much from him in terms of leadership during the past months since the Big Teach, despite Rex's initial lack of interest in the curriculum. But now this all became far more than even personal for Pete. He needed help, so he called in his most trusted advisors. What they had to say didn't surprise him.

When Dr. Dormont heard the group out and shared the information with Ms. Belders, and with Betsy and Sam and with the attorneys, they realized that finding the truth behind the contamination of the water supply and about Paul Sanders' death depended on knowing the whole story from Stevens. How they might get him to talk, they didn't know. As a result of his conviction for shooting at Sam, Stevens had no chance of getting out of prison alive and they couldn't wait that long anyway. Prisoners had strict rights, and they didn't have to visit with parties that repulsed them. The only way to get at Stevens would be to get him to agree to meet. The group decided that it might be effective if Rex and Sam, Betsy, Dormont, Pete and the lawyers asked for a meeting with Stevens. Perhaps he'd bite at the chance to inflict more harm on people he loathed so, and as a result they would get closer to the truth.

They wrote an invitation to Stevens through his lawyers, asking him to meet in order to put their questions and the entire controversy to rest, for the sake of the people involved, and the safety of the entire town.

True to form, Stevens came back with a nasty, scathing letter through his lawyer. Having been advised against even responding, let alone penning a damning note, Stevens mailed the following response to Betsy Sanders:

Betsy, After all these years, I knew, really, that you would get to the bottom of all this. I had no idea that you would put it together so fast, though. You see, this was precisely what I thought would happen if people were left to their own devices to inquire for the truth. But now that I know that you are getting warmer, closer, I'll share with you the details of your husband's demise. It will give me great pleasure to show how evil he was, and how much pain can come from such a timid, weak source. I only make two demands. First, that I get to see Sam in the room so the image of his squirming and bawling through the story of his father's evil–doing will comfort me each night before sleeping soundly. And also that you make the warden of this hell-hole treat me with the dignity I deserve, and get me a private room with decent food to finish out my life. I'll tell the whole story under those conditions. Stevens.

The lawyers met, and they consulted with a judge and the prison warden, and they all agreed that the meeting would take place in a week's time, at noon on a Saturday at the prison in Richway so no one would have to miss school. They agreed to meet Stevens' conditions; they also agreed on a set format for the meeting. Rex Houndson would be allowed to ask Stevens a list of prepared questions. Sam, Betsy, Pete, Belders, Dormont, Missy Tallons, and the Sanders' lawyers could be in attendance, along with Stevens' lawyer.

No one hesitated at the prospects of the meeting, no matter Stevens' capacities for evil and hatred, and his ability to tear down Paul's good name. They knew they must put the case to rest, and get on with their lives. Everything depended on it, the future of their families, their schools, and their community.

66 – IN LOVE FOREVER

Sam and Maggie hung out all week after school. Spring had sprung, and the activities of school and sports and such dominated most of the time they had together, which turned out to be quite often. They spent few minutes apart, which suited them just fine. Maggie had sensed deeply that Sam needed her now. She remembered when he had revealed to her that he would need her very much at some point, that things would get harder as more came out. His intuition had been correct, and now true to her word, she resolved not to leave him high and dry again. She would see this through with him, and love him.

This is a big step emotionally for a 15 year old to take. Sam had taken it long before, but Maggie came to it more slowly. It didn't hurt that Sam made her happy, and that she laughed with him, that she felt alive and cared for, needed, in his presence. After her softball practice and his baseball practice ended at around 5:00 pm, they typically walked to the car and talked and planned for the evening. They would often eat out or with Pete and Betsy, and do their homework together afterward until dark. Lately they had been talking a lot in the barn after hours about how to handle the meeting with Stevens.

On Friday, the night before the Stevens' meetings, Maggie and Sam retired to the barn to read some poetry together after dinner. They had discovered several excellent poets from the early part of the century thanks to Ms. Belders and laughed and talked and wondered out loud as they read the poets what it might have been like to be alive at the turn of the 21st century. After one surprisingly light and airy poem about young love and hope, Maggie surprised Sam with a kiss on the cheek. This time, Sam returned her kiss with a full kiss on her mouth, the kind that means, to a 15 year old, that a deeper desire lurks. Maggie hugged him and kissed him long and hard, responding like Sam had only imagined she might. This delighted them, and brought them closer together. Finally, Maggie held Sam close, his head at her chest, stroking his hair and sharing her beating heart.

She whispered to him, "I will love you, Sam Sanders, no matter what."

He thought about this for a long time, then asked, "But what if it turns out that this whole idea about my father being this great guy and all is a sham? What if my father…?"

"Nonsense," she said, cutting him off before he could go any further, "It doesn't matter anyway. It's about something bigger than us now, and *us* isn't going away."

He kissed her again, and during that kiss, their last one of the night, Pete and Betsy strolled into the barn and turned the halo lights up higher, shouting, "This is certainly a strange lighting mode for poetry reading!"

They all laughed, even though they had been caught red-handed making out in the dim barn light. But the feeling was mutual among all of them, that love should win out, and that the truth might hurt but not separate them further. They said their farewells for the evening, hugging and kissing each other, and crying. Tomorrow would bring a new day, and new relationships. They had come so far and become so close, almost like a new family together. Much was at stake the next day, they knew.

As would be the case for years to come, Sam drove Maggie home in his yellow mustang. And each time he left the house with her at the break of night to return her safely to her father, he made that car churn up the harsh sound of rubber tires biting the graveled driveway. Such sweet music to Betsy's ears.

Morning and the day came fast on Saturday. The Sanders did little different, except to welcome their friends to the house for brunch and the short ride together to the state penitentiary in Richway. This time, however, no crowds or cameras would attend. They had kept the matter rather quiet, except of course to include Missy Tallons from the *Record-Star* to cover the event, just in case a public record needed to be made and shared.

The trip to Richway prison proved uneventful, thank goodness. They emerged from their car and made their way by escort past tight security. They saw no other inmates and few guards as the warden led them to a secure meeting room in a building separate from the main holding area of the prison. After their party got situated on one side of a long rectangular table, split down the middle by a heavy clear plastic window with a speaker phone embedded in it, they awaited the entrance of Stevens on the other side, through a completely separate door.

A guard waited there by a door on the other side of the clear plastic wall, not acknowledging their presence with a wave, a nod, or even a mere look. He only moved when a red light flashed on the bare wall to his left, signaling "prisoner at the door." He turned and opened the door and in rolled Stevens, being pushed in a wheelchair by a prison orderly and followed by his own lawyer from Fletcher, Peter Snaveley. Stevens looked disheveled, his grey hair tousled all about, with his prison orange outfit miss-buttoned and stained from breakfast. Not the picture of health, Stevens slumped in the chair and didn't immediately look up at his audience assembled just feet away, worlds away. In fact, Snaveley spoke first, uncharacteristically.

"Good morning. As you can see, Mr. Stevens isn't well. He agreed to this meeting against my wishes. We must agree before we go any further that anything my client says must remain off the record and not be used against him in any further…"

Before Snaveley could finish, Stevens sprang, "Shut up, Snaveley, what makes you think I give a care what happens to me from now on? Just shut up and take a seat. You'll get paid."

With those short sentences, a reinvigorated Stevens dismissed his lawyer. No one in the room cared to hurt Stevens anymore anyway, he had nothing to fear from them, and he knew it. They just wanted to know the truth, at least his version of it. Somehow, he gathered enough energy to carry the interview.

"You don't care, none of you," Stevens went on, accusing them, "but I'm sick. Cancer. I'll be gone soon. They want to give me treatments here, but I won't have any of it. It's time to be done with this world. Now I know how Sanders felt before he killed himself."

Stevens could hear the gasps on the other side of the wall, and he looked up to see the horror on their faces, especially Betsy's and Sam's. Betsy sobbed, turning her face to the comfort of Pete's chest. Pete pulled her close to comfort and protect her. Sam faced Stevens, steely-eyed though a tear graced his cheek. He was going to speak, but before he could, Snaveley stood up again and spoke.

"I believe you brought some questions with you which my client is prepared…"

But before Snaveley could get his last words out again Stevens snapped, this time he pointing his gnarled, right index finger at Snaveley and screaming, "Shut up, you imbecile! This is my show! Sit down!"

Snaveley, apparently used to these tirades and the pay that came with them, simply held up his hand so as to put distance between him and Stevens, and he sat back down.

At this point, bravely, Rex Houndson opened his folder and spread his question sheets in front of him on the table. He spoke, quivering a bit.

"Mr. Stevens, I'm Rex Houndson. My dad works for you, or at least he did, has for 16 years. I remember meeting you many times at the annual holiday party and seeing you at school board meetings. I just have a few questions that my inquiry group at school keeps bringing up."

He produced a copy of the formula sheets with the scrawlings at the bottom that had become so hotly debated in the class: "Aluminum al Me $." He pressed the paper against the glass so Stevens could see the markings, but Stevens waved him off. He didn't need to see them up close. He knew what they were.

"Put that down, boy. I know what it says."

"What does it mean, Sir?"

"For one thing, it means that you all aren't as ignorant as I thought you were. I thought it would take you at least the rest of my lifetime to figure out how evil Paul Sanders was. But here you are, in flesh and blood while my heart still beats, looking for the truth and red hot on its scent. Impressive."

Stevens coughed a bit, rather violently, to the point that the guard was moved to bring him some water, which he impolitely refused.

"Second, I'll tell you what it means. It's the thing that put Paul Sanders over the edge. He could handle the heat until it came time to shut up and live with the consequences. But he couldn't do it. You see, I had put millions of dollars into the restoration of the plant. Making water was a dream of mine for decades. I got the best intellectual support anyone could find, even among experts," Stevens flashed a cruel, sick smile at Betsy, "and the kind of materials that would last a lifetime or more in order to build it right, and then we found out they were tainted. When we started replacing the pieces, Paul Sanders did outstanding work, making sure that we got every last bit of aluminum out. But at the end of the process, Sanders sent me this note."

At this point, Stevens again coughed, this time violently, even Snaveley came over to check on him, and this time brought water from the eschewed cup to his lips. Stevens accepted it, uncharacteristically, and calmed himself.

He continued, "What it means is that Sanders would agree to keep his mouth shut for money. Keep his mouth shut about what, you ask, young boy?" Now Stevens looked directly at Sam, not at Rex. "Well, the little matter of the exchange station remaining coated in aluminum, that's what. Way deep down in the ground at the core of the conversion operation, at least according to Paul, the exchange station lies buried next to the hydramaster. This is where the elements are combined and cooled all at the same time. Paul knew that it would take millions more dollars to extract the device and either fix it or remake it. But the signs of contamination wouldn't show up for years if we just let it be, unlike the situation with the pipes. I didn't have the money to do this last bit of work, and no one would lend me anymore, so he had me over a barrel. In exchange for his silence, I gave him $500,000 in cash, which he took from me without hesitation. What he did later was rather noble, but really only out of guilt. Trying to start a reading club at the plant was Paul's way of finding out if someone else could figure out that aluminum remained in the system. That was the only way out of his guilt, having someone else find out about the problem, exposing me and not Paul. But I wouldn't have any of it. When he couldn't get it done at the plant, he decided to hide the money in another investment...Belders' library. That place would have gone under years ago if Paul hadn't secretly created a blind trust that supported it. I couldn't stand seeing the legacy of free and open inquiry in that place, but I couldn't do anything about it, like I could by controlling the school board for years and years. As long as I could control the access citizens had to knowledge, I felt like I could keep the plant going and make money and keep our dirty little secrets, secret."

Stevens paused again, this time beaming as he looked at the shocked faces of the Sanders clan through the plastic. For the first time in his life, the truth held power for him and he told it unfettered, freed from his own twisted senses of justice and morality, from the secrets, which were fed by lies and untruths and his own ignorant, selfish, psychopathic self-hatred. The tables turned, this time in his favor, he continued.

"Third, Paul knew there was no way out with the truth. The truth would land him in prison, no matter what. He loved himself more than his child or wife, he told me as much when we met for the last time, he said, 'I can't go to prison, it would kill me.' And it would have. Paul couldn't have stood this place, or the remaining guilt that wracked him. You can go on believing that Paul had an accident that night, but he bought that pole. It was meant for him, purchased by his own guilt and immorality. You answer the question yourself, 'Who extorts the devil himself?' Why, the devil silly. And now, two of us devils are almost dead and gone. And I would have had the third if I could shoot straighter. I never met a more formidable threat than Sam Sanders. I hope that somehow, someday he rots in hell with me and his father. At least you know the truth from both the devils in your lives now. May it give you peace." His facetious grimace finished him off, his energy spent nearly completely, except for a grand exit.

With loathing, then, Stevens whirled his chair around and yelled, "Door, Guard!"

Stunned, Stevens' audience had nothing left to ask, and if it did, no one could muster the composure to ask it. Sick and twisted to the bitter end, Stevens remained in control of his life and the lives of many others. It would take great strength to turn the other cheek, and to walk away from his legacy of evil, the kind that had killed several, and now had truly touched home. Stevens had done his part, turning his back and moving his hatred and evil behind a cell-block. Where would the Sanders and the entire community of Downing put theirs?

What do you say to someone after such devastating news? Nothing really can comfort, not words or acts of kindness, not flowers or chocolates. The Sanders thought they had been through hell before, but now they had to confront the reality that Stevens could be telling the truth and that all of their images and notions of goodness in Paul and his causes had been a sham, covering up, at root, the truth of the matter – that Paul, like Stevens, was an extorting, ruthless, liar.

Betsy herself, however, started the healing by addressing Missy Tallons on the car ride home.

"Missy, you have been so close to us, even as a reporter you have stood by us and helped us tell our story. I want you to report what happened today, and tell the story. There's no use in keeping it quiet. I put all the signs of my life together, and Stevens confirmed what I already suspected could have been the case. Paul kept secrets, I just didn't know they were of such a magnitude. We'll be all right, and this is a forgiving town. We've done nothing wrong. We'll have to trust in our good friends, and move on."

"I'll do my best to tell it right," said Missy.

Silence ensued for many more miles. Then Ms. Belders spoke.

"This story is going to come out, I know it. And I want you all to know that I love you dearly as friends. And that nothing, including these revelations, changes the way I feel, unconditionally, about Paul, and Betsy, and Sam and Pete, too, and everyone else attached to them. We all have flaws. I wish I could have been closer to help Paul work through his secrets and lies, but no one could have if Betsy couldn't have. This just means that this was all much bigger than any of us, and to try to understand it completely doesn't make sense, either. Paul left us a legacy, in Betsy and Sam, and in the library. Sam and his friends will have access to real books for many decades because of him. I know it's all tainted somehow, but now no one else can be hurt by these secrets. Knowledge can free us, and enrich us, I think, especially when it is used for good, sometimes even in the surfacing and dealing with evil. I hope the rest of our lives in this place bear this out."

Belders' eloquence and wisdom soothed the car riders. Several of them smiled at each other, and exchanged loving hugs and touched hands again and again.

They rode in silence the rest of the way home. When the car got to the Sanders' home, another group of people awaited. There stood Maggie and her family, and Ms. Hatcher from the school library, and Mr. Jones from the truants' office. They welcomed them in, with open arms, and then they all joined in to share the sobering news, and ultimately to celebrate the end of a chapter in their history together. They resolved in that place that moving on meant moving on. They would leave the past behind, learn from it, and forge a new future together.

69 – MOONLIT WALK TO FREEDOM

Sam was so happy to see Maggie. But he feared telling her all the truths he had learned that day. He knew she would come to it sooner or later, so on a walk by the pond next to Mr. Frieders' property, which bordered the Sanders Farm, he spilled the whole story to her, crying at times, revealing himself and all of the secrets he could tolerate telling all at once.

In the moonlight, she listened, and held him, and kissed him. She warmed him with her love, everything he needed at that moment, almost 16, a man in a kid's skin, with a lifetime of a good life ahead. She, a young woman, almost 16, turned her insecurities and uncertainties towards Sam and all that he had to bear. She knew that someday, certainly, he would bear her up as well, returning her strength with his. This is what people do when they fall in love. She had learned it from her parents, he had learned it from his. They vowed no secrets that night, and laughed at the absurdity of it all. They cherished the fact that they had found each other. They relished the challenges ahead.

They made their way home that night, late. They walked up the path to the house and saw Betsy kissing Pete goodnight.

"Mom, for heaven's sake."

"We have to move on, Sam."

"See you tomorrow, Pete."

"Good night, all." Pete made his way to his pickup, and sped off, throwing gravel as he went. Betsy smiled, and Sam knew she would be happy again.

Sam drove Maggie home after everyone else had gone. He kissed her goodnight, too, and said he was looking forward to being back at school with her Monday. Monday came quickly, as it always does.

The story spread around town and school very quickly. Dr. Dormont called a Big Teach to tell her version of things and to invite questions. Students all around Sam gasped at the news, at first, but then their reservations and disillusionment turned to support and good wishes. People had been hurt in that town, by Stevens. No one had perished because of Paul's actions, they all knew that, though they also recognized his recklessness and his greed, though ultimately the resources had served the causes of good. They were willing to suspend judgment on Sam and Paul and the rest so long as they too could move on with security and freedom, which were guaranteed by their teachers and Dr. Dormont and their families.

Dr. Dormont quickly turned them to the next task at hand, which was to somehow pull together all that they had learned that year for presentation to the Justices of the State Supreme Court, especially Chief Justice Haskins. While the Justices had shown great confidence and support in them, everyone in that school knew that a great burden attached to their public showing. The justices could either write them off as a failed experiment and restore the former school regime including the standardized curriculum and testing system, or use their case as support to help other districts break from the stranglehold that the testing and accountability movement had placed on public schooling for more than 30 years. They had only a few weeks of working time left before their big day. They made the best of it.

First, students split themselves up by into study groups to examine the wealth of data that they had accumulated that year in terms of student records of achievement: books read, topics covered, lessons taught, projects created, papers written, etc. They grouped all of the data under four categories, four main themes that they felt captured their learning for the year: Life Choices, Social Justice, Real Science, and Organic Tension. The main thread, of course, was the school's search for truth surrounding the mystery of the water plant, all the parties involved, and the potential for re-contamination of the water supply. Thankfully, the threat had been headed off with all the information that had come to light. The filters had been put back to work, taking out any deadly aluminum that remained, and the plant had finally been sold to a new company that vowed to remove the tainted exchanger and make the necessary repairs to update the plant and keep people working.

Rex Houndson wouldn't admit it, so his classmates did it for him: they built in the story of a reluctant student, who did more than merely stumble luckily onto a crucial set of data and facts, but instead worked diligently on important tasks and came to see the possibilities of inquiry. Rex, like many others, had strong, inquiring minds that got used very little in school before the revolution. Now, it became routine for them to take on issues and problems and work ethically through various modes of inquiry to get at the truth. In manners reminiscent of now well-known journalists like Missy Tallons, they worked tirelessly toward the truth of the matter at hand, because it is the right thing to do, and the heritage of a free society bent on laying the foundation for justice, equity, and freedom for all.

71 – A LAST HURRAH

Weeks of preparation flew by. School time seemed to fly, like there wasn't enough of it. This constituted a dramatic change in how things typically felt for students in Downing at the end of a long, painstaking, drudgery-filled school year behind the same, tired computer terminal. But this year had been a whole different story. It didn't feel like there was nearly enough time to do everything that they wanted to do in class and in the world. Nonetheless, because they stuck tirelessly to their tasks, the students and the teachers felt ready for the presentation, but how would the justices react? What precedent guaranteed that the school had met the judges' standards? What were their standards?

Buses filled with students and teachers and parents made their way to Richway on the last day of school. Once again, the atmosphere felt circus-like, with reporters with cameras for cinevision all around, telling their side of the story for a now inquisitive public.

When the courtroom finally filled with the students and the luminaries and the press, the Justices came in one by one, just like they had late last summer. And this time, Chief Justice Haskins spoke first, again:

"Welcome back, Downing. This is a festive occasion. We want you to treat it as a great success. Please don't worry about our decision, it's already been made. Thanks to Missy Tallons, we have a pretty good idea about what went on in your town the past months. We believe that you deserve a round of applause from us for your diligence and courage. So before you tell us your story for the next hour, we offer you this."

And one after the other the judges rose and applauded the town assembled in their room. This town that had overcome secrecy, and disease, and greed, and hatred – together – with children at the forefront, got their heartfelt and genuine applause. Missy Tallons said later that "I nearly fainted when I saw it happen. No judge applauds for anyone, anytime."

Somewhat shaken, but spurred on by the judges, Sam Sanders rose to make an opening statement, his last before the court:

"Thank you so much for welcoming us to Richway. Ours is a story of gain and loss. I lost my father several years ago. He got tangled in a huge mess at the plant in Downing with his boss, Mr. Stevens. I lost everything, or so I thought, when he crashed his car into a tree on his birthday, all alone, just a few years ago.. But thanks to my friends and colleagues at school and in the community, I've got a new lease on life, a new outlook. My interest in finding out more about the world has been better served by schooling than it was before Judge Haskins' order last summer. This year we spent our time and energy looking for answers to burning questions that we had. Our teachers spent time planning together and talking about ideas. What it all led to was a complex set of connections and possibilities for growth that we never would have come close to recognizing had we all been stuck behind a computer terminal the whole year, like machines, simply learning a rote, standardized curriculum. Instead of studying 'westward expansion' and the 'industrial revolution' we talked about cultural and human genocide, greed, and industrial waste. We found out firsthand what can happen when money becomes more important than human life, and saving one's assets becomes a game of Russian Roullette with other people's lives. So, today we want to show you what we know about the world. Rex Houndson, Leader of Team 1, will start off explaining how we organized our learning activities for the year with our teachers. Thanks so much for supporting us and our learning."

Sam Sanders sat down, clutching Betsy's and Maggie's hands, and Pete put his arm on the boy's shoulder. They sat back, then, much more relaxed, and watched the past year unfold for them through the eyes of the students and the teachers who had learned so much right along with them. This time, no police cruisers rumbled up to cart off books or to chase Dormont from the building. No, Downing School would be open for a long time, as long as the spirit of free inquiry in support of creativity and imagination and ethics in learning and teaching held center stage over standardization, control, and discipline. Still, only time would tell, since there was always next year now, with new challenges for teaching and learning, and new questions, tasks to tackle, together, with confidence and yet deep uncertainty. In the end, they relished the prospects of such endeavors and of tomorrow, creeping up to meet them and their new lives.